100 YEARS OF THE
BULLS

100 YEARS OF THE
BULLS

Telegraph & Argus

breedon **books** PUBLISHING

First published in Great Britain in 2007 by
The Breedon Books Publishing Company Limited
Breedon House, 3 The Parker Centre,
Derby, DE21 4SZ.

© Telegraph & Argus, 2007

A catalogue record for this book is available from the
British Library.

ISBN 978-1-85983-604-0

Printed and bound by Cromwell, Trowbridge, Wiltshire.

Contents

Foreword

Like many stories, the history of Bradford Bulls (and their predecessors, Bradford Northern) has humble origins. And there are moments – pivotal ones – where, had decisions gone the other way, the club as we know it would not now exist: dark days, certainly, but days of incredible joy too.

That is the nature of sport, both on the field and, more often than not, off it. And that is the nature of the history of Bradford's top rugby league team.

The first part of our book takes you on this journey, explaining how the club we now know came into being. In travelling this path, there is also much to learn about the city, its history and the people who live, and have lived, in it.

The second section focuses on the people who crossed the white lines and carved out a piece of immortality for themselves, the players who, week in, week out, were the dream-makers for thousands of fans. You may argue about our choices, agree or disagree with our reasons, and put forward your own favourites. For that is the beauty of sport.

We are indebted to JOHN DOWNES, Heritage Development Officer, of the Bradford Bulls Foundation, and MARTIN BASS, Assistant Heritage Development Officer, who are both long-standing supporters of the Bradford club. John and Martin have combined their talents to write a definitive history of the club and the personalities and players that have helped shape it over the last 100 years.

These dedicated fans – Martin is a former supporters' club chairman – have also trawled through the club's archive and the library of the *Telegraph & Argus* to source hundreds of momentous and revealing photographs, many unpublished for decades.

The links between club, fans and city are complex. The Bulls could never have happened anywhere else: they helped shape the very place of their birth, altering our sporting and cultural landscape forever. They have helped forge, too, our identity as a city and others' views of us – and for the better.

Where they go from here is a matter of hard work, hope and fate, but the *T&A* will be there to cover the pride and the glory, the triumphs and the disappointments. The fans will be there, too, to roar them on and history will, again, be on our shoulders.

Perry Austin-Clarke
Editor
Telegraph & Argus
August 2007

Chapter 1 Prequel to a Centenary

It might come as a surprise to some but the roots of Bradford Bulls lie in social football played to Rugby School rules. Indeed, the club have a shared genealogy with both Bradford & Bingley RUFC and Bradford Park Avenue AFC.

Although Bradford Northern were formed in 1907, the heritage of the club goes back to 1863, 10 years before the town hall was built, to the formation of Bradford FC, which changed its name to Bradford RFC in 1866. The club was the brainchild of Oates Ingham, who owned Lingfield Dyeworks near Four Lane Ends, in Thornton Road.

Bradford's first home was at Horton Cricket Club, whose ground stood roughly where St Luke's Hospital stands today. However, after only two years the rugby club were asked to leave because of damage to the pitch. The club led a nomadic existence, using six different homes in six years, before finally settling at Apperley Bridge in 1874.

During 1879 the Bradford Cricket, Athletic and Football Club was formed and they built a new ground at Park Avenue. After much debate, Bradford RFC merged with the new Park Avenue sports club.

The first rugby match was played at Park Avenue on 28 September 1880, when Bradford lost to Bradford Rangers. It took place on a section of the cricket pitch and it was not until 1884 that the cricket and rugby fields were properly segregated.

By the beginning of the 20th century, all four sides of the rugby ground had been developed. It was capable of accommodating large attendances; crowds of 20,000 and 18,000 saw Bradford take on their wool city rivals Manningham in Yorkshire Cup ties of 1884 and 1886.

Bradford became one of the leading clubs in the country, providing many players for Yorkshire and England.

By the late 1880s the rugby world was showing signs of stress over the issue of 'broken time' payments for working-class players. Eventually this led to rugby's great schism in 1895, when 22 of the north's leading clubs broke away to form the Northern Union, now known as the Rugby League. Within two years of the split, nearly half the membership of the Rugby Union had joined the new organisation. The Bradford club were reluctant members. Several members determined to stay within the RU broke away from the Park Avenue club to form Bradford Wanderers RUFC who, after several mergers and name changes, became Bradford & Bingley RUFC.

Despite the switch to the Northern Union, Bradford's finances were under strain. Large debts were incurred with the purchase and development of the ground.

Overleaf: 1898 Challenge Cup finalists, left to right, back row: E. Airey (hon. treasurer), E.R. Hoyle (secretary), F. Lister (N.U. rep), A.H. Briggs (chairman). Third row: R. Holt, R.J. Robertson, T.H. Dobson, W. Murgatroyd, J.W. Fearnley, S.R. Rhodes (committee), J.T. Toothill. Second row: R. Wood, J. McLoughlin, T. Broadley (captain), H. Holden. Front row: E. Kelsey, H. Prole, F.W. Cooper, F. Murgatroyd, B. Patrick. This Bradford side lost 7–0 to defending holders Batley at Headingley, Leeds, in the second ever Challenge Cup Final on 23 April 1898.

Bradford NUFC 1898–99, left to right, back row: Robinson, W. Murgatroyd, Calvert, Pollard, Toothill, Radcliffe, Fearnley, Wright. Middle row: Prole, Kelsey, Robertson, Dobson, Cooper, Broadley (captain), Wood, Holden, Booth, Holt. On ground: F. Murgatroyd, Patrick.

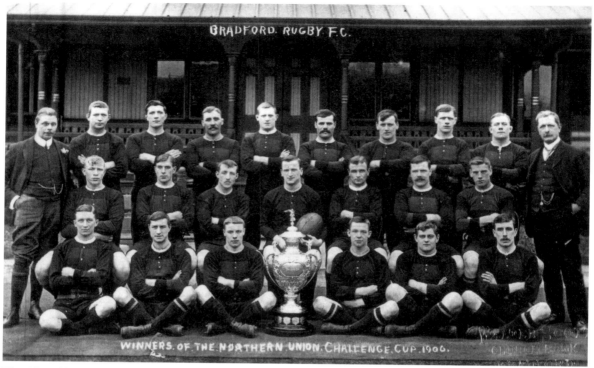

The 1906 Challenge Cup winners.

However, a period of sustained success began to slowly ease these debts. Between 1895 and 1906, the side never finished in the lower half of the league, winning three championships. In 1906, the club won the Challenge Cup and, in the final season at Park Avenue, Bradford won the Yorkshire Cup.

However, the 1906–07 season saw the club marooned in 18th place in the league and suffering the worst financial losses in their history. It was a combination that was to lead to one of the most controversial periods in Bradford's sporting history.

Indeed, 1907 was the most significant year in the history of Bradford sport. Bradford Northern and Bradford Park Avenue AFC were born and Bradford City almost abandoned their Valley Parade home. It was a year that was to define Bradford sport for a century.

The tumultuous year began with an assurance from the English Rugby Union that the Bradford club would be welcomed back into the fold, but not the players who had turned professional. In February, letters were sent to all the members asking what they thought the club should do to survive. The replies were split between riding out the current difficulties and reverting to Rugby Union. Tellingly, there was not a single suggestion that the club should follow the lead of former rivals Manningham, who had been transformed into Bradford City AFC.

However, behind the scenes the committee had already approached its counterpart at Valley Parade with a view to marrying the successful City side with the excellent facilities of the Park Avenue ground.

On April 15, 300 members attended a hostile meeting where they were initially asked to vote on three proposals:

Should Northern Union (Rugby League) continue?
Should the club revert to Rugby Union?
Should the club adopt Association Football?

The Mayor, Alderman J.A. Godwin, presided over the meeting and, after heated debate, changed the initial vote to Rugby or Association. Rugby won this first ballot with a considerable majority. The next issue to sort out was English Rugby Union or Northern Union. A return to English Rugby Union won the day.

Barely a week later, the club's solicitor declared that the members' decision was null and void because a general meeting could not be held in April. It was a flimsy excuse, and on the very same day the committee of Bradford City agreed to consider a merger. In this game of bluff and counter-bluff, and almost certainly as a bargaining chip, Bradford applied for admission to the Football League as Bradford AFC.

However, a Valley Parade defence committee quickly sprang up among the City supporters. The debate centred on identity and a concern that the Park Avenue club were

Bradford Northern Football Team 1907-8

The first picture of a Bradford Northern team, 1907–08.

trying to take over the successful City team. The fiery eloquence of the fans won the day as the City members rejected the amalgamation by 1,031 votes to 487.

Undeterred, Bradford's all-powerful finance and property committee voted 18–2 to change to Association Football. When the Football League rejected Park Avenue's application, the board responded with an audacious bid to join to the Southern League. It was accepted and Bradford (Park Avenue) AFC was born.

On 24 May a meeting of Northern Union supporters was held at the Mechanics' Institute. Presiding over the meeting was Cephas Rhodes, a mill manager from Great Horton, who was determined to see the game continue in the city. During the evening, many impassioned speeches were made condemning the management of the club at Park Avenue. A provisional committee was to begin making arrangements for a new club to be formed and to seek a new ground.

The committee consisted of Messrs Cephas Rhodes,

Ezra R. Halford, J.E. Dobson, T.E. Riley, F. Crowther, W. Peel, W. Rawson, R. Fitzgerald, W. Banks and W. Robinson, with Mr R. Hinchliffe as secretary.

On 26 June the first annual meeting of the new club was held, thus saving professional rugby in Bradford. Mr E. Halford chaired the meeting and the following committee was elected: Messrs W. Murgatroyd, J.E. Dobson, E. Halford, S. Neumann, R. Robinson, W. Banks, S.J. Whiteley, W. Peel, R.H. Rawson and W. Bayliss. Mr C. Hepplestone was elected president.

A Bains card from around 1910 depicting **Bradford Northern**.

The club moved in at Greenfield Stadium and played their first match against Huddersfield on 7 September 1907, losing 5–8 before a crowd of between 4,000 and 7,000. The club thought that the Bradford public might be unaware that Northern Union football was still alive in the city and so the suffix Northern was added to the name before the next match.

Cephas Rhodes later became club chairman, a position he held until resigning on 21 May 1915, at the club's AGM. During that meeting it was announced that the club had amassed large debts in the preceding year (the club still owed money on a previous loan, with a £62 repayment due in June). Cephas launched a blistering attack on his fellow directors, claiming they were not pulling their weight and leaving it all to him. He was fed up with what appeared an impossible position and sadly resigned immediately.

Chapter 2 Birch Lane

After spending the first year away from Park Avenue at Greenfield Stadium, the club took the bold step of moving to Birch Lane, where the rent was £30 a year, compared to £8 at Greenfield. The club had rejected Birch Lane the previous year because of a prohibitive rent of £50. The perceived advantages in moving were that the ground was nearer to the city centre, had better transport links and was located on a direct bus route with a neighbouring tram terminus and a railway station only a short walk away. Another significant advantage of the new venue was the potential for development. The committee believed an upturn in playing fortunes would bring back the crowds. In 1908 an optimistic Bradford Northern moved home for the second time in two years.

Within a short time this optimism turned into despair

Bradford Northern, 1913.

BRADFORD NORTHERN (RUGBY) FOOTBALL TEAM.

as Northern's tenure at Birch Lane saw the club endure one of the worst periods in its history. A Yorkshire Cup Final appearance in 1913 was the closest the team got to winning anything. After a dour struggle for survival during World War One, the cessation of hostilities failed to lift the gloom. The club were about to embark on a 15-year journey of despair, finishing bottom of the league five times and second from bottom six times. The only glimmer of hope came in 1927–28 when the side climbed up the table to the dizzy height of 16th, 13 places above the bottom.

Northern were living hand to mouth, week to week. On numerous occasions the Rugby League had to bail the club out with handouts. This depressing period saw the club in the headlines for all the wrong reasons:

1919 – the club were in trouble with the league for not paying transfers;

1921 – a directors 'coup' (it would be nice to call it a boardroom coup but the club were too poor to have a boardroom);

1926 – the Birch Lane ground was closed because of crowd violence;

1927 – Northern were taken to court over non-payment of bills;

1928 – a players' strike;

1931 – beaten by Leigh's A team (there was a players' strike at Leigh).

The desperate situation at Birch Lane is illustrated by the club's activities in the transfer market, where, it appears, a policy of signing former greats was employed. Jack Bartholomew, a member of the first touring side in 1910, played for Bradford between 1914 and 1922; Jack Beames, a former Test player signed from Halifax, was temped out of retirement at 33,

Alfred Mann, second row or prop. He had two spells with the club in 1905–09 and 1919–22.

Teddy Melling played from 1920 to 1928, staying loyal through the dark days at Birch Lane.

making 24 appearances before finally retiring; and Stanley Moorhouse, a former international, was signed from Huddersfield, but played only five games, in 1923/24. Former Bradford favourite Alf Mann, who was sold to Hull KR in 1909, was brought back in 1919 and played until 1922. The legendary Albert Rosenfield, who scored a record 80 tries in 1913–14 for Huddersfield, signed in 1923, playing 23 games before retiring in 1925, scoring only a solitary try in Northern colours. Harold Young, signed in 1926, became the first Bradford player to tour in 1928. Immediately after returning he was sold to Huddersfield, returning to Birch Lane in 1933, two

Bradford Northern, at Birch Lane, 1920.

years before his retirement. Local lad Stanley Brogden made his debut at 17 and notched up 62 appearances before being sold to Huddersfield for £1,000 to alleviate financial pressure. He returned to play 33 games during World War Two. The popular Teddy Melling was one player who played during his peak. He was signed in 1920 from Batley and made 286 appearances, scoring 339 points in eight years. Due to the persistent financial crisis at the club, he was sold to Broughton Rangers for £300 in 1928.

In early December 1929, the Rugby League decided that enough was enough. Drastic action was required. Consequently it sent a team of three to take over the running of the club for one month and assess whether the club had a future. Money was made available, allowing the club to fulfil all fixtures. Other clubs were informed of Northern's dire situation. Several offered players on a loan basis. Some clubs helped by holding

Len Dobson, second row or prop. 1912–26.

A Bradford Northern programme cover for their game against Batley, 12 November 1921.

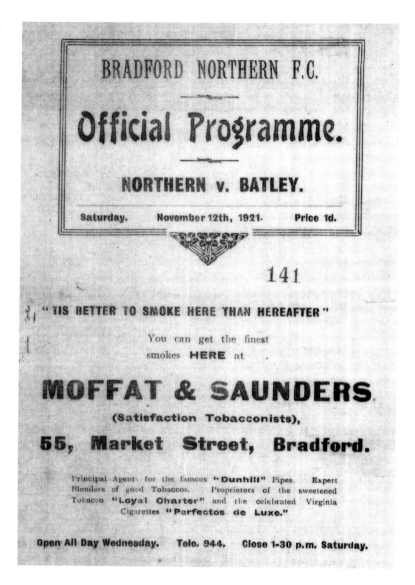

collections on match days. Within 10 days an almost entirely new team took the field against Leeds and 12 days later, on Christmas Day, Northern secured their first win of the season. Off the field, the league representatives had persuaded six local businessmen to join the existing board. Although improvements on the pitch were negligible, the club was starting to build a little stability.

Amazingly, in 1933, Northern achieved one of the most remarkable results in Rugby League history by defeating the touring Australians. For the Kangaroos, the result of the match against the Birch Lane club,

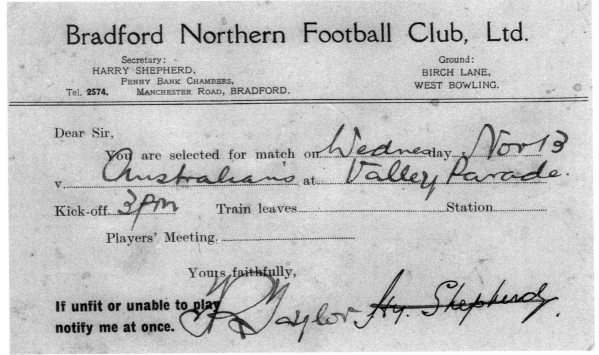

Bradford Northern Football Club, Ltd.

Secretary:
HARRY SHEPHERD,
PENNY BANK CHAMBERS,
Tel. **2574.**   MANCHESTER ROAD, BRADFORD.

Ground:
BIRCH LANE,
WEST BOWLING.

Dear Sir,

    You are selected for match on......*Wednesday Nov 13*......day

v.......*Australians*......at......*Valley Parade.*

Kick-off....*3pm*......   Train leaves......................Station........................

Players' Meeting........................

        Yours faithfully,

**If unfit or unable to play
notify me at once.**   *Taylor Hy Shepherd*

**A selection card for the match
against the visiting Australian
team.**

which was one of the game's perennial strugglers, was a forgone conclusion. The tourists' record was played 12, won 11, the only defeat being the first Test Match the preceding Saturday. Their wins included impressive victories against Lancashire and Yorkshire.

Due to the poor state of the Birch Lane pitch, the game was moved to Valley Parade for a Wednesday afternoon. From the kick-off the tourists were back-pedalling due to the ferocity of Bradford's forward play and the crowd of only 3,328 could sense the chance of an upset. By half-time, Northern were still in contention with the score 5–5.

The second period produced a titanic struggle in the mud and, with every Bradford tackle and pass being cheered on by the partisan crowd, the Aussies failed to make any advantage. The referee awarded a scrum 15 yards from the Aussie try line. Bradford, feeling confident, employed the tactic of only packing down with five, second row Sherwood standing in the loose. Northern, incredibly, won the ball. As it came out of the scrum, Bradbury passed to Sutton, who sent the ball on to Sherwood in space. The Aussies tried to reach the second row as he kicked a drop goal, leading to chaotic scenes on the terraces. With only enough time to restart the game before full-time was blown, Northern had secured the shock of the century, winning 7–5.

The humiliated Kangaroos demanded a rematch. This was arranged for 30 October. The fixture, also played at Valley Parade, was another tight encounter, with the outcome being determined by a disputed try scored by the tourists with three minutes to go.

The good feeling generated by this chapter in the club's history could be the reason for their gradual rise from no-hopers to champions within the next decade. The first positive move after this mini series was the signing of Tom Winnard, a centre from St Helens, who cost £385. After years of selling their best talent, the board of directors, by signing Winnard, had shown its intentions. Tom became the bedrock on which the club's revival was built. He played for 10 years, making 253 appearances and becoming the first Northern player to score 1,000 points.

Chapter 3 Hole in the Ground

Before the move to Odsal in 1934, Bradford Northern's very existence was continually in doubt as the club struggled from one financial disaster to another. No matter how hard the club fought, success or even stability was not to be found. The club lived hand to mouth, week to week, survival being the only tangible achievement over the 26 years spent at Birch Lane.

Several times the Rugby League had to bail the club out of the fiscal mire that accompanies failure on the pitch. To compound the problems on the field, the ground was regarded as one of the worst in the league. With no money to spare, the stadium, which lacked basic facilities, gradually fell into a desperate state of disrepair. The only way out was a fresh start at a new home.

In the early 1920s, under the directorship of Ernest Call MBE, the Bradford Cleansing Department had devised a system of tipping refuse which was to

The 1925–26 squad, left to right: F.D. Mereweather (trainer), F. Kirkham, E. Brett, R. Hughes, E. Gledhill, C. Agar, E. Melling, F. Gomersall, H.B. Shaw (director), J. Mills, H. Webster, J.C. Davy (director), L. Dobson, J. Moran, C. Redman, H. Smith. The two gentlemen to the right are unknown.

transform desolate areas into pleasant playing fields and gardens. Many such places are still in use today, including Bradford Grammar School playing fields, King George V playing fields and Bankfoot cricket field. This revolutionary method of tipping would eventually be used through out the world. One of Mr Call's more ambition schemes was to build a stadium capable of holding 150,000 spectators utilising controlled tipping in the old quarry where the Richard Dunn sports centre now stands in the Odsal valley.

The Odsal valley used to run from the quarry down to the Spen valley. Initial work started at Odsal to a master plan detailed on a diagram dated 26 August 1930, which included a unique three-storey pavilion, which had changing rooms at pitch level and a ballroom and bar at the level of the Rooley Lane concourse. From Nigel Williams's book we can only assume that this grandiose scheme (the first of many such schemes) was abandoned by the local authority. The council continued

The Bradford Northern team at Birch Lane on 21 September 1929, which lost 2–5 to Salford. Back row, left to right: Hume, W. Sherwood, Thorner, Cox, Sykes, Dolan. Front row: Sims, J. Sherwood, W.R. Smith, Reed, Jones, Gledhill, Woodruffe.

to tip at Odsal with the aim of completely filling the whole void.

At an early stage of the above development, Mr Marshall, a Bradford Northern director, came up with an idea similar to Ernst Call's original plan, where the amphitheatre created by the tipping could be used as a stadium. On 27 April 1933 the club officially approached the council with this initiative. The proposal was agreed by the council after a survey of the site. All parties met on 20 June to discuss terms for what was no more than a hole in the ground. Northern agreed a 10-year lease at an annual rent of £20, plus 1.5 percent of gross revenue of gate and car parking. The rugby club would have to erect all exterior fencing, changing facilities and seating accommodation, taking control of the 'stadium' on 1 January 1934.

When the club took control of Odsal, the site consisted of a vast bowl created by controlled tipping. The club's three main priorities were the levelling and laying of the playing area, the erection of a stand for spectators and the building of changing facilities.

The directors came up with a novel idea for solving the first of these problems, with the announcement of the Odsal turf scheme, in which supporters could buy a piece of turf on behalf of the club, an 18in x 12in (400mm x 300mm) piece for 6d (2.5p). For this plan to work, 49,500 pieces needed to be sold to create a playing area of approximately 110yds x 82yds. As an incentive to subscribers, a grid map showing the name of each person next to the location of a piece of turf was to be publicly displayed in the club house. The public response was exceptional, raising nearly £900 of the £1,237 target. The grid map never materialised.

Bradford Northern, 1932–33, wearing chevron jerseys. They were one of the first teams to wear this design, which later became synonymous with Rugby League. Back row, left to right: Thornburrow, Parr, Elson, Litt, McLester, Taylor, Sutton. Front row: Townsend, Walker, Bradbury, Smith, Sherwood, Bush.

As the start of the season loomed, with time and money running out, the club needed to build a perimeter fence and a grandstand. The Rugby League came to the rescue by loaning the club £2,000, enabling the work to go ahead. The stand was constructed on the area where the dressing rooms are today. It had only a modest capacity of 2,000 and was completed only a day or so before the first match.

Controlled tipping to create the playing area at Odsal in 1933.

Odsal, late September 1935. The terrace takes some shape.

Odsal, September 1935. The clubhouse and terrace houses still stand in 2007.

An Odsal Stadium Grand Opening Ceremony ticket.

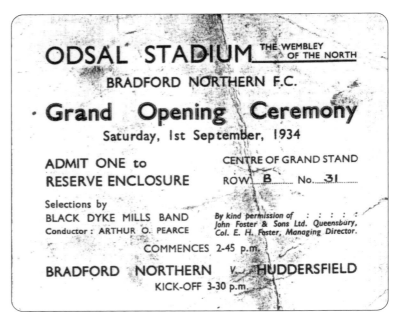

The stadium itself was very primitive, with only a few rows of railway sleepers around the pitch and the slopes created by the tipping as terracing. Within the first year, the railway sleepers were to be covered by tipping.

It seems inconceivable nowadays that a stadium of such magnitude could be constructed without the use of concrete. Amazingly, this glorified hole in the ground was being hailed as the 'Wembley of the North'; tickets for the first match against Huddersfield optimistically

Bradford Northern, 1934–35.

carried that slogan. Contemporary reports of the stadium's opening mention the vastness of the place compared to the claustrophobic conditions of Birch Lane. Spectators were amazed at how small the players looked from the top of the banking. Everybody recognised the potential that had yet to be realised fully. Council tipping within the bowl continued throughout the first 10 seasons!

Northern fared no better than at Birch Lane, losing 16–32 in the opening match against Huddersfield. The new surroundings had minimal effect on performances with 10 straight defeats. Northern broke their home duck at the seventh attempt with a 15–2 victory against Featherstone Rovers.

Action from the 1935–36 season. C.L. Grainge is on the burst at Odsal. Note the state of the stadium and the length of the grass.

Chapter 4 Post-war Boom

With the move to Odsal came a gradual improvement on and off the field. A general feeling of optimism began to emerge from the doom and gloom of the Birch Lane days.

Within the first year at their new home, Northern had secured the signatures of George Carmichael, Vince Dilorenzo, Stanley Orford and Ted Spillane. The charismatic visionary Harry Hornby arrived just after the move to Odsal to become the chairman and managing director. One of his first major appointments was the recruitment of Dai Rees as coach, who continued to acquire players. Just two weeks after his arrival he signed Ernest Ward on his 16th birthday. George Bennett and George Harrison were signed from Wigan.

Willie Davies is welcomed to Odsal by Harry Hornby and Dai Rees.

Professional tennis at Odsal in 1936. Note the small size of the banking at the east end of the ground and the view of Odsal Woods, later to be used for tipping.

By 1937, the club were on the rise, a fact reflected in attendances. In August 1938, Willie Davis was on board. September saw the legendary Trevor Foster join and, in December, Frank Whitcombe arrived. A great team was emerging when world events overtook the Rugby League scene: World War Two broke out.

The club were determined not to let the war derail the progress made. Dai Rees realised what needed to be done if Northern were to continue the march towards being a major force. He would only use, where possible, bona fide Northern players, as opposed to 'guest' players. This philosophy paid great dividends, the club winning seven major trophies throughout the war years. However, Rees did take advantage of guest

Big Frank Whitcomb clears his line.

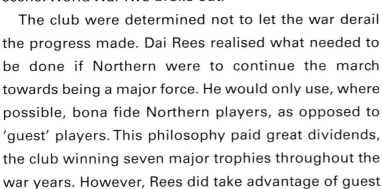

The Northern line up on 25 May 1940 versus Swinton. Back row: Foster, Smith, Jenkins, Harrison, Higson, Winnard, Lambert, Whitcombe. Front row: D. Ward, Dilorenzo, Moore, Carmichael, Hayes.

players without disrupting the progress of the club. For example, the great Gus Risman, then of Salford, played eight times in 1940–41, and the legendary Jim Sullivan made an appearance as full-back against Halifax in the Challenge Cup third round of 1941–42.

The euphoria that swept through the country at the end of World War Two was carried through in Bradford for a few years longer due to the success of the Rugby League club. Peace-time brought a bigger stage, with

Donald Ward covers as Huddersfield look to break away.

Donald Ward chases the ball through.

huge numbers flocking to every match as the public soaked up every bit of entertainment available after six long years of hostilities.

Northern established themselves in the upper echelon of the game, mainly with the same players who

Donald Ward about to be tackled in a wartime match at Odsal. Other Northern players are L. Higson and W. Hutchinson.

Total confusion in a match against Huddersfield at Odsal in 1946.

A Bradford Northern programme from 1946.

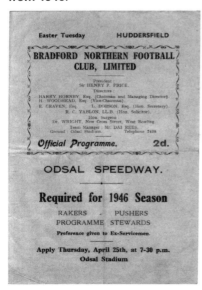

had brought success throughout the war years, becoming, under the captaincy of Ernest Ward, the first team of any code of football to appear in three successive Wembley Finals, winning two. A narrow semi-final defeat against Widnes in 1950 prevented a fourth visit to the Twin Towers. Two Yorkshire Cup triumphs and a Championship Final completed this glorious period in the club's history.

In the first season after the cessation of hostilities, Northern became ironic victims of their own strength when six players were selected to tour for Great Britain. Foster, Whitcombe, Ernest Ward, Kitching, Batten and Davies left on 4 April 1946, on board the aircraft carrier HMS *Indomitable*, with 10 league games still to play. Naturally the club's standing in the league slipped. From leading the table they dropped to fourth, earning them a trip to Wigan in the Championship semi-final that, not surprisingly, ended in defeat.

The three Wembley Challenge Cup campaigns all

astonishingly started with first-round defeats. Thankfully, in those post-war days, the first round was played over two legs. The talent within the Odsal ranks is illustrated by the fact that in each of the three Finals a Bradford player collected the Lance Todd trophy as Man of the Match. Frank Whitcombe became the first forward and first member of a losing team to collect the honour with his blockbuster performance against Wigan in 1948.

In each of the Finals, the world-record attendance for a Rugby League match was broken, rising from 77,605 at the 1947 Final against Leeds to a Wembley sell-out against Halifax in 1949 of 95,000.

It is hard to describe the difference between the build-up to a Wembley Final in austere post-war Britain and one in today's consumer society. Supporters prepared for the Finals by knitting scarves and bob hats and making paper rosettes. There were no replica shirts in those days as rationing and clothing coupons were still in use. A popular supporters' accessory was a former

Northern return with the Challenge Cup in 1947.

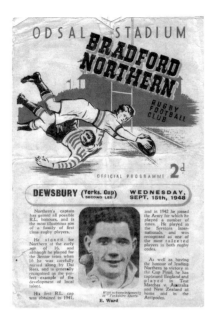

air-raid warden's rattle, painted in club colours. Fans would have had to save up for the relatively expensive trip to the far-off capital. Bear in mind that a coach trip to London in pre-motorway England could take eight hours. The newly nationalised British Rail laid on special trains from various points in Lancashire and Yorkshire – mainly day trips as a weekend away would be out of the reach of most. An estimated 20,000 to 30,000 followers left Bradford, bound for Wembley, complete with club favours, home-made sandwiches and a Thermos flask.

In 1947, the victorious team returned to Bradford on the Monday for a civic reception at the Town Hall. Tens of thousands turned out to give the side a tumultuous welcome, the sheer numbers bringing the entire city centre to a standstill, repeating the jubilant scenes outside the Town Hall on VE Day, only two years previously. This public celebration was to be repeated two years later when Northern returned home after beating Halifax at Wembley.

Ernest Ward shows the trophy to the crowd in Town Hall Square, 1949.

The players proudly display the Challenge Cup after beating Leeds 8–4 in the 1947 Wembley Final.

Wembley 1947

On the Saturday the journey to Wembley was not without incident, as the coach driver lost his way in London. Frank Whitcombe, Northern's burly prop forward, a lorry driver by trade, saved the day by taking over the wheel and delivering the party to the Empire Stadium only 30 minutes late. Leeds started as 6/4 favourites, having reached Wembley without conceding a single point. The match itself was a typically hard Leeds–Bradford derby game. The Leeds pack at the time was known as the Super Six. To combat this threat, Dai Rees instructed scrum half Donald Ward to operate at dummy half because of his ability to dispatch long passes to keep the play away from the formidable Leeds forwards. The Bradford pack operated a man-for-man marking system. Northern's handling was reported to be smooth and fast and several good try-scoring opportunities were missed in the first half, the only score of the half being a penalty in the Lioners' favour.

The second period after the initial exchanges saw Leeds's Super Six on top until a fast break and quick handling move, followed by a long pass from Kitching to Ernest Ward, created an overlap for Emlyn Walters to score the first try. The conversion was missed and within minutes Leeds regained the lead with a penalty. Ernest Ward surprised everybody with a drop goal to restore the advantage. In the latter stages, with the Leeds defence in total disarray, Trevor Foster walked over for a try, the last score of the match, making it 8–4. Willie Davies completed the day by picking up the Lance Todd trophy as Man of the Match.

Wembley 1948

Just seven days earlier Northern had beaten Wigan in an epic championship semi-final at Central Park. At Wembley the Pie Eaters exacted their revenge, winning 8–3. Fate appeared to be against the Odsal outfit from the start, as Eric Batten's attempted clearance was

The king shaking hands with Northern's captain Ernest Ward before the kick-off of the 1948 Cup Final at Wembley. Other players are, left to right: Leake, Batten, Case, Edwards, Davies, D. Ward, Whitcombe.

charged down by Wigan winger Jack Hilton, who dribbled over the try-line before dropping on the ball. Ted Ward converted the score. Northern hit back straight away, with Ken Traill kicking to the corner for Alan Edwards to touch down for Northern's only score. As chance after chance went begging, it seemed that it would not be Bradford's day. Wigan's Brian Blan dribbled a drop-out back to the Northern line before prop Frank Barton pounced on it to complete the scoring in the second half. For those who believe in fate, Northern's nine-year-old mascot Tony Halliday was not allowed to lead the team out onto the hallowed turf as it was against the Empire Stadium rules. Even a letter to King George VI, who was guest of honour, could not reverse the ruling. Whenever Tony had led the team out during the season, they had never lost. The distraught schoolboy had to make do with watching his heroes lose from the stands.

1948 Cup Final action. Barry Tyler is held by a determined Wigan defender, while Donald Ward and Frank Whitcombe move in to support.

Overleaf: the 1949 Rugby League Challenge Cup winners, left to right: B. Tyler, J. Kitching, T. Foster, E. Ward, K. Traill, E. Batten, F. Whitcombe, A. Edwards, R. Greaves, B. Leake, V. Darlison, W. Davis, D. Ward.

'We've done it again!' Ernest Ward and Donald Ward celebrate after securing their third successive Wembley Final, after beating Barrow at Swinton in the semi-final.

Northern's Challenge Cup semi-final side that beat Barrow 10–0 at Swinton in 1949. Back row: Foster, Radford, Batten, Greaves, Kitching, Tyler. Middle row: Darlison, Leake, E. Ward, Edwards, Traill. Front row: Davies and D. Ward.

Wembley 1949

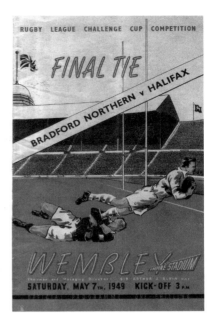

On Northern's third consecutive visit to Wembley there would be no mistake. Against local rivals Halifax, the much larger and more mobile pack dominated from the start, hooker Vic Darlison winning 42 of the 55 scrums. Winger Eric Batten made up for any mistakes 12 months earlier by refusing to leave the field after fracturing his shoulder in the opening minutes when scoring the first try after chasing an Ernest Ward kick. Ernest converted, taking the score to 5–0. Amazingly, Northern failed to improve the score even though they totally dominated possession. After the break, possession turned into points, first with a penalty and then with a clever move between Donald Ward and Ken Traill sending second row Trevor Foster over to score. Ernest Ward converted to make the scoreline 12–0, giving Halifax the dubious honour of being the only rugby team to fail to score at Wembley.

As with any sport in any period, success was due to a combination of factors. Northern achieved it through their collection of remarkably talented players, melded into a team by visionary coach Dai Rees.

It is often said that the cornerstone of any great Rugby League team is the pack. This was true of the Bradford six. Formidable as the pack was, only Welsh

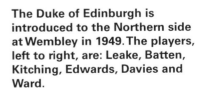

The Duke of Edinburgh is introduced to the Northern side at Wembley in 1949. The players, left to right, are: Leake, Batten, Kitching, Edwards, Davies and Ward.

Donald Ward passes inside to Ken Traill, with winger Eric Batten to his right against Halifax at Wembley in 1949.

prop Frank Whitcombe topped 18 stone, a weight that would prove very useful given the high number of scrums in those days, and he would help hooker Vic Darlison to heel the ball.

With Odsal legend Trevor Foster in the second row and stylish Ken Traill at loose forward, the backs had plenty of ball to show off their skills. The wing pairing of Edwards and Eric Batten, famous for leaping over his opponents, capitalised on the openings created by their centres, Jack Kitching and captain Ernest Ward, the 'Prince of Centres'. Stylish Willie Davis and Donald Ward at half back displayed an array of tricks that bamboozled their opponents. Many older followers of the club still rejoice in the deeds of the post-war period.

Souvenir booklet from the 1947–49 Challenge Cup Finals.

Chapter 5 To Oblivion

In the middle of the 20th century, Bradford Northern slipped from the pinnacle of the sport into oblivion. As the public became more affluent, from post-war austerity to the Swinging Sixties, carpets replaced lino and Bradfordians wanted more than windswept cinder terracing and a failing team. Over a depressing nine-year period, club attendance fell from a club record 69,429 for a Challenge Cup quarter-final against Huddersfield, to a pitiful 324 against Barrow in 1963.

By 1952 the post-war boom that had benefitted all spectator sports was in decline. Unfortunately, at Odsal, the team was also in decline. In 1952–53, Northern were still a major force in Rugby League, finishing third in the

The new floodlights are tried out at a training session in 1951.

Previous page: Downpour! The result of a thunderstorm at Odsal in August 1952.

league and playing in front of the club's record attendance of 69,429 for the Challenge Cup quarter-final against Huddersfield. The following campaign saw the Yorkshire Cup won, although a moderate league position of ninth (out of 30) was considered a poor season. By mid-September 1954, the supporters believed the previous season was just a slight dip in form, having started the new campaign with nine straight wins. Sadly the team could not maintain that kind of form and slipped to 17th position.

1955–56 saw a mediocre Northern finish eighth in the league. Nobody could know then that the old Northern would only appear in the top half of the table once more, in 1957–58.

The drop in fortunes on the playing front was coupled with an alarming decrease in attendances, inevitably leading to financial problems. In 1953, the club showed remarkable pettiness in not allowing Ernest Ward's move to Castleford as player-coach without a transfer fee. He had given the club 14 years of loyal service and Northern did not want him to join their coaching staff. Perhaps this was the first sign of the poor financial state of the club.

With gates dwindling from 1952 onwards, by 1957 the

Bradford Northern, 1951–52, league leaders. Back row: Foster, Shreeve, N. Haley, Mageen, Smith, Traill, Radford, Tyler. Middle row: Jenkins, Seddon, Hastings, Ward, Phillips, McLean, Hawes. Front row: L. Haley, Goddard, Dickson and Greaves.

Northern team photograph, 1956.
Back row: Scroby, Belshaw,
Jones, Mackie, M. Davies,
Radford. Front row: D. Davies,
Ward, Mageen, Lancaster,
Hambling, Smith, Seddon.

club were in talks with the stadium owners, Bradford
Council, about a rent reduction. After considerable
negotiations, the council offered Northern a three-year,
rent-free loan of the ground providing Northern paid
£50 a day or 10 percent, which ever was the higher, of
any takings generated by non-rugby league activities at
Odsal. At the time, speedway took place at the stadium.
The Northern board refused the deal. By December
1957, Northern had sunk further into a financial morass
that convinced the board to accept the council's offer,
which meant a saving of £3,750 over three years.

By 1960 the club was well and truly established at the
bottom of the league table. Dai Rees, who had coached

Players' Christmas party, 1959,
held in the club house, now used
as the club's main office.

Northern team photograph, 1960. Back row: Robbins, Marston, Doran, Winnard, Hemingway, Kosanovic, A. Dawes. Front row: Trumble, Davies, Higgins, Greenall, L. Haley, B. Smith.

Northern through the highly successful 1940s, was relieved of his duties on 22 March 1960, and replaced by Trevor Foster. Rees was given the job of maintenance manager of Odsal stadium, a very strange appointment. The club had claimed on numerous occasions that while money was scarce, the stadium did not need anybody to run it full-time.

Supporters and shareholders were becoming angry and frustrated at the constant sale of players, players who, if they had stayed, could have improved the standing of the club. Storey went to Featherstone, Traill and Scroby to Halifax – the latter for a then club record fee of £7,500 – Kosanovic to Wakefield (£2,000), Derek Davies to Leeds (£5,750) and T. Robinson to Bramley

(£6,000). The transfer that enraged supporters the most was the sale of Malcolm Davies to Leeds for £3,000 in January 1957, just five months after signing him from Leigh for £750. Instantly the gates fell by 1,800 as the public showed its aversion by staying at home. The whole philosophy of selling the best players brought back memories of the Birch Lane days.

By the start of the 1957–58 season Davies had returned to Odsal. He became a crowd favourite as he ran in tries at a phenomenal rate in a struggling team. In total, he played 96 games, scoring 91 tries. On his return to Bradford he was employed to run the pools scheme, which became very successful, generating vital revenue for the club. The board were not impressed, however, by the fact that he was taking a commission. On his departure in 1960 the pools scheme collapsed, depriving the club of vital income when they needed it most.

By 1961–62, Northern had sunk to new depths,

Team picture with Trevor Foster as coach. **Back row: Crabtree, Radford, G. McLean, M. Davies, Foster (coach), Scroby, B. Smith, Kosanovic. Front row: Hemingway, Winnard, G. Haley, Seddon, L. Haley (captain), D. Davies, Jenkins, Jones.**

finishing bottom of the league for the first time for 30 years and recording their worst-ever defeat, 73–5 at Wakefield in the Yorkshire Cup. The club was in a terminal spiral of poor results, falling crowds, decreasing income and lack of investment, which inevitably led to large debts. With the league dividing into two divisions for the 1962–63 season, Northern's prospects appeared even worse, with no big derby matches and not much hope for improvement on the field. Again Northern finished bottom of the league.

With no investment by the directors, who were either unwilling or incapable of raising capital, the outlook for the 1963–64 was not encouraging. With only one win to their credit, on 14 November first-team coach Harry Beverley resigned and refused to give any reason for his decision. On 23 November, two days after President Kennedy's assassination, the club had its lowest ever attendance, against Barrow: the writing was on the wall. Without any capital the club could only manage to fulfil one more fixture, which was against Leigh at Odsal on 7 December.

One of the last Northern sides before the collapse in 1963. Back row: Abed, Doran, Hardcastle, Crabtree, Wigglesworth, Gomersal, Hume. Front row: Davies, Reynolds, Haley, Beevers, Carr, Coggle.

The never-ending battle with financial troubles came to an inevitable conclusion on 10 December 1963, when the bank refused to loan any more money. The council did try to save the club but, with little money coming through the turnstiles and no funds from the pools, the sad decision was taken to go into liquidation. The *Telegraph & Argus*, Bradford, reported on the front page:

END OF THE ROAD FOR NORTHERN
Money Difficulties.
'Can't go on' – Chairman.

In November 1963, the crowd for the match against Barrow was a pitiful 324 in a ground that only nine years earlier had hosted a world record crowd of 102,569 for the Challenge Cup Final replay between Warrington and Halifax. The final match against Leigh attracted 841, with an estimated 500 travelling from Lancashire.

Before the demise of the old club, the battle to re-form Bradford Northern had begun. Trevor Foster had formed a consortium to keep professional rugby league alive in Bradford.

Chapter 6 Back in Business

On 14 April 1964, 1,500 Bradfordians sat in hope and trepidation in St George's Hall for the meeting that galvanised the support for the new Bradford Northern club. Trevor Foster and former playing colleague Joe Phillips had formed a consortium to create a new Bradford Northern and the response to the meeting generated an unstoppable momentum.

The backing of the council, local businesses, the

rugby league community and supporters had helped Northern to put together the bones of a team at virtually no cost. Odsal Stadium would continue to be the home of a rugby league club.

Who would have thought that just four months later the club would be lifting their first trophy as winners of the Headingley Sevens and beating hosts Leeds along the way? The first season saw team-building continue and within 12 months the club had produced the Yorkshire Cup winners of 1965. For the rest of the 1960s, Northern consolidated their position.

Bradford Northern playing squad 1965. Back row: Rae, Lord, Hepworth, Hill, Fearnley, Smith, Potter, Levula, Batty, Williamson, Ackerley, Crawshaw, Roberts, –?–. Middle row: Clawson, Brown, Ashcroft, Davies, Stockwell, Hardcastle, Smales, Ashton, Morgan, Walker, Rhodes, Brooke, Hirst. Front row: Metcalfe, Scattergood, Breakespeare, Butterfield, Sutcliffe, Carr. A. Sutcliffe and Riley were on holiday.

Headingley Sevens winners, 1964. Back row: Brian Lord, Idwal Fisher, Johnny Rae, Mick Brown, Jack Wilkinson (coach). Front row: Derek Carr, Keith Williams (captain), Ian Brooke, Joe Phillips (chairman), Brian Todd.

The Lord Mayor of Bradford, T.E. Hall, is introduced to the Bradford Northern team prior to their first game after re-forming in 1964.

Northern cheerleaders.

Northern suffered a temporary dip in 1973, slipping to 23rd in the league, a position that would condemn them to the newly-formed second division despite appearing at Wembley in their first Challenge Cup Final for 24 years. Unbowed, they bounced straight back into the first division as champions, with 24 victories from 26 games.

Northern players go down the steps to take the field against Keighley.

Prop Ken Roberts is hauled down by a Hull KR man in the mud at Odsal in 1968. Berwyn Jones is in support.

Terry Clawson receives his Man of the Match prize from the 'John Player' girl.

The 1970s seemed to be a constant battle with rivals Widnes, as the clubs clashed in five major Finals or semi-finals, with Northern victorious in two John Player Finals and a Premiership Final. As coach Peter Fox's team developed into the double championship winners at the turn of the decade, Northern were to be Yorkshire

Wembley, 1973. The players are, left to right: Tees, Lamb, Stockwell, Watson, Redfearn, Blacker, Seabourne, Hogan, Dunn, Earl, Joyce and Pattinson.

The 'Tiller Girls' of Odsal prepare to set off for Wembley in 1973.

Barry Seabourne is tackled by the Featherstone defence at Wembley.

RUGBY LEAGUE CHALLENGE CUP COMPETITION

FINAL

BRADFORD NORTHERN

VERSUS

FEATHERSTONE ROVERS

SATURDAY 12th MAY 1973 — WEMBLEY STADIUM JUBILEE 1923-1973 — Kick off 3 p.m.

OFFICIAL SOUVENIR PROGRAMME . . . TEN PENCE

The 1973 Challenge Cup Final programme.

Wembley disappointment for David Treasure.

Cup winners again, beating York, but also suffered the heartache of losing a Challenge Cup semi-final and Premiership Final to Widnes and another Premiership Final to Leeds.

It's milk all round as Northern celebrate their Premiership win in 1978.

Bob Haigh holds up the Premiership Trophy outside the Town Hall.

Disappointed Northern players after losing the 1980 Premiership Final to Widnes. From left to right: Garry Hale, Jeff Grayshon, Steve Ferres, Les Gant.

Northern began the 1980s as champions and became only the third team in history to retain the championship in 1981. The following season, Northern became infamous for their 'walk-off' protest at Hull Kingston

Keith Mumby is carried by jubilant fans after Northern secured the 1980–81 League Championship.

1981 Rugby League Champions. Players celebrate after clinching the title. Left to right: Steve Ferres, Alan Redfearn, Derek Parker, Alan Parker, Dennis Trotter, Phil Sanderson, Jeff Grayshon Graham Idle, Jimmy Thompson, Tony Handforth, Jim Fiddler, Les Gant, David Redfearn, Garry Van Bellen, David Barrends, Keith Mumby, Nigel Stephenson, Peter Fox (coach), Gary Hale, Ronnie Barritt (physio).

Rovers in the first round of the Premiership play-offs. Five players had been sent off by half-time and Jeff Grayshon's dismissal after 58 minutes sparked a protest which was to see Northern fined £4,000 and banned from all 1982–83 season Cup competitions except the Yorkshire Cup. This ban was later suspended for three

Jubilant players enjoy a civic reception with the Lord Mayor after retaining the League Championship in 1981.

The Steam Pigs!

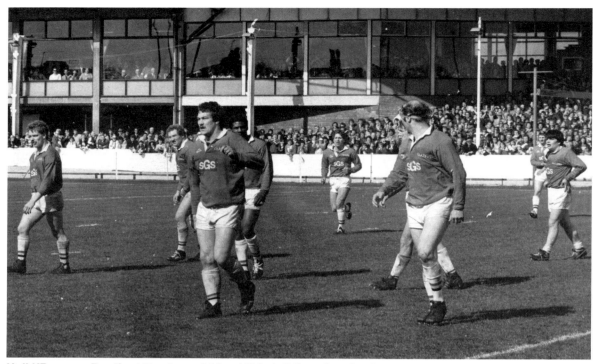

Hull KR versus Bradford Northern, 3 May 1982. Jeff Grayshon leads his men from the field in a 'walk-off'.

Sparks fly as Grayshon and Millington clash.

years after appeals from both club and supporters.

The championship was to be the last success for the club in the early 1980s with Yorkshire Cup Final losses in 1981 and 1982 together with a Challenge Cup semi-final loss in 1983, which included an Ellery Hanley try remembered more than any other by many Northern fans. It was 1987 before success was to

Jeff Grayshon powers through the Fulham mud at Craven Cottage.

come in the shape of a replayed Yorkshire Cup Final at Elland Road when Northern beat Castleford. The decade ended with further Yorkshire Cup success in 1989, with a 20–14 win against Featherstone Rovers.

Northern celebrate their Yorkshire Cup win against Castleford. Back row: Roebuck, Mumby, Stewart, Simpson, Skerrett, Hobbs, W. Heron, McGowan, Ford, D. Redfearn. Front row: Mercer, Fairbank, Hill, Noble, Harkin and coach Barry Seabourne. Mascot Ben Noble.

Noble looks on as a Hull player receives a mighty tackle.

Ivan Henjak and Gerald Cordle celebrate the Yorkshire Cup win.

The 1990s would turn out to be as chaotic as any decade in the club's history. At the end of 1989–90, a season that saw three different coaches at the helm, Bradford's nemesis of the late 1970s, Widnes, struck again, with a 28–6 win in the Premiership Final at Old Trafford. The Cup Final frustrations continued with losses in the 1991 Regal Trophy Final and the following season's Yorkshire Cup Final, while the side slid into the relegation mire. Peter Fox returned to stop the rot, saving the club from the ignominy of relegation.

Unfortunately, Northern had to suffer the humiliation of a record defeat of 71–10 at the hands of Wigan in the

The Flying Fox (Deryck) scores his first try for Bradford.

Simpson scores at Valley Parade.

Young Bradford Northern supporters.

Northern centres Shelford and Newlove model the new kit.

Karl Fairbank tries to evade a Wakefield tackler.

1992 Challenge Cup semi-final. There seemed to be some hope of championship success in 1994 when the title appeared to be within Northern's reach, but a home defeat at the hands of bottom-placed Leigh meant that only a win at Wigan's Central Park ground could resurrect the title bid. It was not to be, however, and a

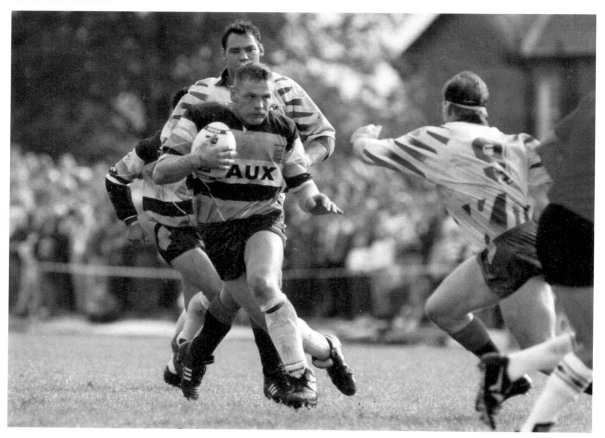

Northern celebrate a big Headingley win. Back row: D. Heron, Watson, Shelford, P. Grayshon, Hamer, Fairbank, Clark, Powell, Dixon, Hall, Newlove. Front row: Nigel Stephenson, Holding, Summers, Cordle. Sitting: D. Fox.

Premiership semi-final loss to Castleford brought the season to a disappointing end. The mid 1990s were also mid-table time for the team.

In the League Centenary season, 1995, Bradford Northern transformed themselves into the Bulls with surprisingly little opposition. By the time Super League arrived, the Odsal outfit had completely redefined themselves from a traditional rugby league club into a family-oriented, community-based Super League franchise complete with razzmatazz.

Jon Hamer surges forward for Northern.

Chapter 7 Birth of the Bulls

Visionary chairman Chris Caisley saw the advent of Super League as an ideal opportunity to develop a completely new approach both on and off the field. Innovative coach Brian Smith was recruited from Sydney, and he appointed compatriot Matthew Elliott as his assistant. The centenary season prior to the start of Super League was used as a trial and building period as Brian Smith used over 40 players while establishing structures that would stand the club in good stead for years to come.

Twenty-three players were signed in the 12 months, and the transfer of international centre Paul Newlove to St Helens brought the trio of Bernard Dwyer, Paul Loughlin and Sonny Nickle, who soon became the foundation of a new team. With cash to spare, other players were brought in: Paul Cook, Matt Calland, Jon Scales, Simon Knox and, from Australia, Graeme Bradley and Jerry Donougher.

As the winter Centenary season fizzled out, the Challenge Cup started. Fate was on the Bulls' side, with

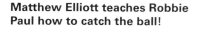

Matthew Elliott teaches Robbie Paul how to catch the ball!

Bulls fans celebrate their semi-final victory over Leeds.

relatively easy ties against lower-division sides before they were pitched against old rivals Leeds in the semi-finals. The 28–6 victory catapulted the Bulls into the public's consciousness, creating the ideal climate for the launch of Super League.

The Wembley-bound side opened their Super League campaign with a 30–18 win against Castleford at Odsal in front of 10,027 spectators, over twice the previous

Robbie Paul celebrates the 1996 semi-final win with fans.

Jimmy Lowes and Paul Loughlin enjoy the victory over their closest rivals in 1997.

Bulls fans on the Wembley trail.

season's average. Not even a Wembley defeat, 32–40 to St Helens, could halt the momentum of the Bulls phenomenon.

James Lowes, Steve McNamara, Glen Tomlinson and Stuart Spruce were brought on board. A final position of

Dejected Bulls players after losing to St Helens at Wembley in 1997.

third was just a stepping stone on the way to future success. Brian Smith departed, leaving Matthew Elliott to lead the Bulls to the Super League championship in 1997. A record start of 20 victories led to another Wembley trip, which unfortunately ended in defeat, 22–32, against St Helens. The Super League title was clinched at Sheffield Eagles' impressive Don Valley stadium in front of thousands of travelling Bradford fans with three games to play. The presentation of the trophy took place at Odsal the following week after the thrashing of Paris St Germain 68–0 in front of 16,761 ecstatic supporters, amid an unforgettable party atmosphere. The Bulls had arrived.

Off the field, marketing guru Peter Deakin arrived to spread the word about what was happening at Odsal. He transformed unfashionable Bradford Northern into

Steve McNamara kicks for goal.

Jeff Wittenberg scores the championship-clinching try at Sheffield.

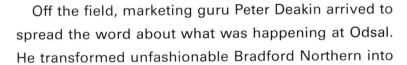

Robbie Paul lifts the Super League trophy in 1997.

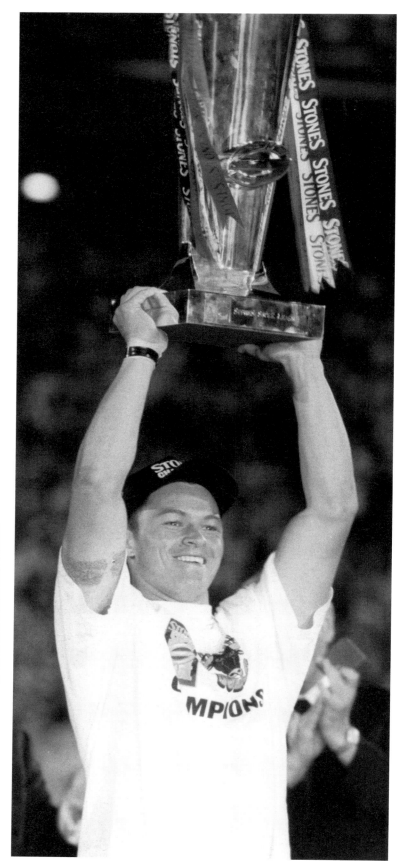

Super League Championship celebrations.

Bulls fans celebrate victory at the Don Valley stadium.

brand leaders. Gary Tasker, the company secretary who later became chief executive, drove this new philosophy forward and implemented a five-year, market-led plan. Marketing manager John Hunt revolutionised the club merchandise, further enhancing the brand. The Bulls logo soon became one of the most recognisable emblems in sport.

With the new image came a new focus for the club – the family. The Bulls recognised the importance of their position as part of the community. Schools and community groups were contacted and both coaching and lifestyle message assemblies on topics such as teamwork and healthy living were delivered to groups all over the city and beyond. Literally thousands of people, young and old, have been 'touched' by the Bulls over the years. The Bulls have been recognised by local and national politicians as having played a significant part in bringing the diverse sections of the community together in a common aim, and what could

Gary Tasker (Bulls general manager) one of the architects of Bulls' early success.

John Hunt, Northern's commercial manager, the man behind the Bulls' early merchandising.

Tevita Vaikona strides out of St Hilaire's tackle.

be more of a focus than a sports club bearing the city's name?

Super League III began with even higher expectations with the arrival of Great Britain legend Shaun Edwards. Unfortunately, 1998 proved to be slight stutter. The signing of the prodigious scrum half did not work out and, after a disappointing first half at Salford in round 11, Shaun disappeared into the dressing rooms, never to return in Bradford colours. An early exit from the Challenge Cup and a final position of fifth did not halt the progress of the Bulls, as once again they proved to be the top crowd pullers.

With the arrival of Australian full-back Michael Withers and Robbie Paul's brother, Henry, coupled with the emergence of young prop Stuart Fielden and three-quarter Leon Pryce, 1999 was destined to be an eventful year. The Bulls breezed their way to the Challenge Cup

A young Stuart Fielden signs for the Bulls.

Bradford Bulls smash their attendance record with a gate of 24,020.

semi-final, only to lose to a revitalised Rhinos. In the Super League, the Bulls clinched top spot and the Minor Premiers title with a Withers drop goal in the final minute of a sensational 19–18 win over Leeds, in front of a Super League record crowd of 24,020.

The play-offs saw a stunning performance as Bradford secured a Grand Final place by crushing St Helens 40–4 in front of an ecstatic Odsal crowd. The

A record 24,020 fans packed Odsal to see the Bulls beat Leeds 19–18.

St Helens v Bradford Bulls, the JJB Super League Grand Final.

Bulls had finished five points above Saints in the table and looked set to lift the Super League trophy when Henry Paul opened the scoring with a 60-yard solo effort which he converted. Leon Pryce had a 'try' controversially ruled out by the video ref, Withers being judged to have knocked on in the build-up while Saints had no points. Sadly St Helens took control of the match, winning 6–8.

The new millennium saw club captain and crowd favourite Steve McNamara leave for Huddersfield to be replaced by Australian Brad Mackay. The Bulls started at a blistering pace, winning the first 11 matches including the Challenge Cup Final in Edinburgh. The cup campaign was no fluke and the Bulls beat Super League opposition in every round, finishing with a 24–18 win over the Rhinos at Murrayfield. The match will be remembered

The 2000 Silk Cut Challenge Cup Final programme.

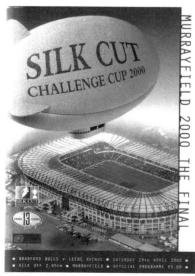

The Bulls celebrate their win.

Tevita Vaikona with cup.

for Henry Paul's pin-point field kicking, which earned him the Lance Todd Trophy, and Nathan McAvoy's chip and catch over Leeds full-back Harris to score the Bulls' final try before half-time. The victory saw the cup return to Bradford for the first time in 51 years.

Form slipped in the later stages of the season, leaving the Bulls in third place and with a trip to Saints in the play-offs. A tight 16–11 win was rewarded with a home derby against Leeds in what was to be Odsal's last match until 2003. The Bulls eased past their neighbours 46–12 before succumbing 12–40 to Wigan in the final eliminator. For the 2003 season the Bulls were to use Bradford City's Valley Parade ground while Odsal was being redeveloped.

The Bulls arrive back from their win over Leeds at Murrayfield.

Chapter 8 Exile at Valley Parade

In 2001, the Bulls vacated their Odsal home after 67 years to play at Bradford City's Valley Parade ground. The move was to allow the council to develop Odsal Stadium.

On the field the success continued, with the Bulls serving up an exciting, mouth-watering, free-flowing style of play. Sadly, the move was not popular with the supporters. The club's tenure at Valley Parade coincided with the Manningham riots. Family-orientated supporters felt negative about the temporary ground and subsequently attendances fell by an average of 2,911 per match.

Henry Paul tries a pass watched by Saints' Kevin Iro.

Mike Forshaw is taken down by two Saints players.

Henry Paul after the Challenge Cup Final.

The team easily qualified for another Challenge Cup Final, this time at rugby union's headquarters, Twickenham. St Helens would once again provide the opposition in what should have been the 'dream' Final, as the teams occupied the top two positions in the league and had scored the highest number of points. The game turned out to be a damp squib, played in pouring rain. Each team cancelled out the other's attacking flair and Saints, who were becoming Bradford's latest nemesis, took the match 6–13. In Super League, the Bulls took the Minor Premiers title in style, trouncing Leeds 68–18 in the final match.

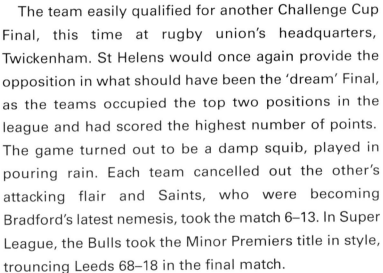

Bulls fans at Old Trafford for the Grand Final against Wigan.

Michael Withers running through the Wigan defence in the Grand Final.

The Grand Final programme.

Opposite: Graham Mackay with the Grand Final Trophy.

The Bulls took the quick route to the Old Trafford Grand Final, beating runners-up Wigan at Valley Parade. How can Bradford fans ever forget that magical Manchester evening, when Michael Withers scored a hat-trick of tries before half-time? The impressive 37–6 mauling of the Warriors gave the Bulls their second Super League title – memories to savour.

2002 started with Bulls winning the World Club Challenge against Australian champions Newcastle Knights 41–26. Very shortly afterwards the club was brought back down to earth when Leeds dumped them out of the Challenge Cup at the first hurdle at Valley Parade. The Bulls had the little distraction in mid-season of competing in rugby union's Middlesex Sevens, taking the tournament and trophy by storm against the best that union had to offer.

In Super League, Bradford's attacking style earned

James Lowes and Brian Noble at the World Club Challenge.

James Lowes with the World Club Challenge trophy after Bradford beat Australian champions the Newcastle Knights.

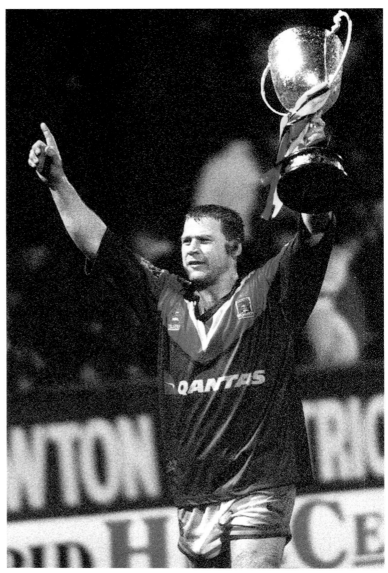

Members of the Bulls squad to take part in the Middlesex Charity Sevens at Twickenham. Michael Withers, Rob Parkin, Jamie Peacock, Lee Gilmour, Nathan McAvoy, Lesley Vainkolo, Robbie Paul and Tavita Vaikona

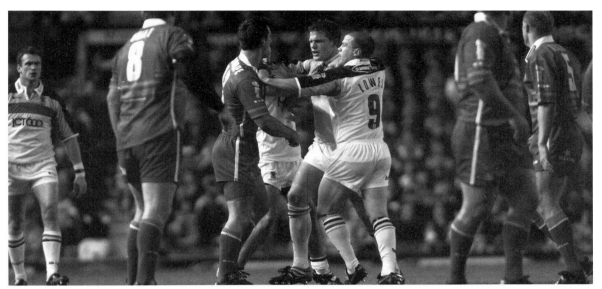

them second place and an away tie at St Helens' Knowsley Road fortress in the play-offs. A decisive 28–26 victory sent the Bulls back to Old Trafford to defend their crown.

In one of the most controversial Finals ever, a Sean Long drop goal two minutes from time gave Saints an undeserved 19–18 coup. After taking the lead after three minute through a Naylor try, the Bulls were denied a Deacon try under the posts. Referee Russell Smith handed over the decision to the video referee, who made the wrong judgement by deeming that Peacock had knocked on in the build-up. Over 60,000 spectators at Old Trafford and a television audience of millions knew the verdict was wrong. Whether St Helens could have come back from that score is debatable. Worse was to follow in the last minute when Saints' captain, Chris Joynt, took a voluntary tackle in front of his own post just after Long's drop goal. Sensationally, no penalty was awarded so the spoils headed for Merseyside.

Prior to the play-offs, Bulls chairman Chris Caisley, disillusioned with the council's failure to fulfil its the promise to develop Odsal, started negotiations for the club to take over the stadium, carry out the necessary improvements and return home for the 2003 season.

Stuart Fielden is restrained by his teammates as he tries to go for a St Helens player in the first half of the Final.

Mike Forshaw pulls down a St Helens player.

Paul Deacon salutes the fans after the defeat.

The Bulls return to Odsal.

Chapter 9 Return to Odsal

The Bulls had relocated to Valley Parade to accommodate the building phase of the Odsal development, to be carried out by the council in partnership with Leeds-based Stirling Capital. Even a 6,000-signature petition in support of the scheme could not stop the scrapping of the project. At the heart of the plan was a retail development which included a Tesco

supermarket. This raised various objections from, among others, Bradford-based Morrisons. The Secretary of State for Transport, Local Government and the Regions, Mr Steven Byers MP, intervened by calling for a public inquiry. Because of the time and money and uncertainty caused by such an inquiry, the investors, Stirling Capital, and Tesco, pulled out, leaving the proposal high and dry.

For the Bulls, the thought of continuing in Manningham was unpalatable. Chairman Chris Caisley

Gareth Gates coming out of the tunnel as the Bulls celebrate returning to Odsal.

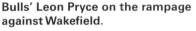

Bulls' Leon Pryce on the rampage against Wakefield.

took up the fight and publicly badgered the local authority. After accusations and counter-accusations from both parties, a deal was struck. The Bulls returned to a modernised Odsal. The main stand was refurbished, with nearly 5,000 seats and a new roof, new concourse bars were built, the old toilet blocks were replaced and modern, high-powered floodlights were installed. On 9 March the Bulls returned to their spiritual home. A two-storey corporate hospitality stand was completed within a couple of months.

On the field the members of the squad that had come so close to being crowned champions were retained, with the addition of utility player Karl Pratt from Leeds. Youngsters Leon Pryce, Stuart Reardon, Paul Deacon, Jamie Peacock and Stuart Fielden were to stamp their mark on the game. Lesley Vainikolo and centre Shontayne Hape developed into one of the most lethal partnerships in Rugby League.

The significantly large crowd of 20,283 showed its

support for the return to Odsal as the Bulls defeated a stubborn Wakefield team for their first 'home' victory for two years. A winning run developed that saw Bradford reach the Cup Final in Cardiff, as second in the table, to face leaders Leeds.

The Final, played at the magnificent Millennium Stadium, lived up to all the pre-match hype as the derby rivals battled tooth and nail for the first trophy of the season. The game had every thing that a derby match should have.

Leeds captain Sinfield created the biggest talking point by famously electing to not 'take the two' near the end, which would have tied the Final at 22–22. The match ended in total confusion when a spurious hooter sounded minutes before the final hooter, as if the game had not had enough drama in the preceding 80 minutes. As in Edinburgh three years earlier, Bradford were worthy winners. The victory was to complete a unique treble for Bradford: they are the only club to win the Challenge Cup in three different countries.

Bulls' Jamie Peacock scores the winning try.

The victorious Bulls Challenge Cup Final team.

Opposite: Robbie Paul celebrates winning the Challenge Cup against Leeds in Cardiff.

Form slipped a little after the Final, but with three league victories over nearest rivals Leeds, the Minor Premiership was secured with a game to spare. Each of the three league derbies had as much drama as the Cardiff encounter. Who could forget that a month after the Final, this time at Odsal in front of 21,784 spectators, the Rhinos were blown away 48–22, with the most talked about incident being Paul Anderson's hand-off on Gary Connolly before touching down for a try.

Crowds gather for the Challenge Cup Final homecoming.

The next tussle saw Leeds proudly sitting at the top of the table. Another bumper crowd had gathered for the showdown. Leeds flung everything at the injury-ravaged Bulls that humid evening at Headingley. The Bulls' defence held firm, typified by young Stuart Reardon tackling Danny McGuire when the entire Leeds fans had thought he was through as the final hooter sounded.

The fourth clash was to decide the destination of the Minor Premiership and proved to be the tightest of matches, settled by a Deacon drop goal two minutes from the end. The Bulls, having finished top, had the advantage of a week's rest before entering the play-offs. The Rhinos were the opposition again, so, for the fifth time in a season, the two West Yorkshire giants clashed. Again the Odsal team proved too purposeful, with a combination of guile, skill, pace and power, for the men from LS6 and a 30–14 victory ensured another visit to Old Trafford.

The Grand Final saw Wigan attempt to prevent the rampaging Bulls from completing the treble. After taking an early six-point lead, the champions-elect clawed their way back into the game with two penalties just before half-time. The second period saw the Bulls

Joe Vagana lifts the Super League trophy.

Bulls' Stuart Reardon scores his try against Wigan in the Grand Final.

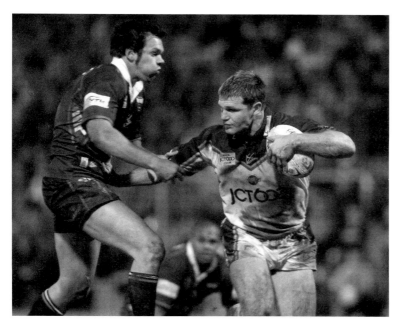

Stuart Fielden knocks Penrith's Luke Rooney away – and the Bulls go on to win the World Club Challenge 2004 at the McAlpine stadium in Huddersfield against Penrith Panthers.

run away with the game, culminating in a trademark James Lowes try, converted by Paul Deacon, taking the score to 25–12. With victory, Bradford Bulls became the first team of the modern era to complete a clean sweep of domestic honours.

The trophy hunting didn't stop at Old Trafford. Season 2004 saw the Bulls, after a couple of friendly games, win their second World Club Championship, beating Aussie champions Penrith Panthers 22–4 at Huddersfield's McAlpine Stadium.

With four pieces of silverware in the trophy cabinet, the Odsalites started their defence of the domestic title by thrashing Wigan 34–6, powerhouse winger Lesley

Michael Withers takes a kick for the Bulls in place of injured Paul Deacon.

The Bulls celebrate winning the World Club Challenge 2004.

Bradford players Jamie Langley and Paul Johnson (above), and captain Robbie Paul (below) look disheartened as their team falls to the Rhinos.

Bradford fans are disappointed by the team's performance against the Rhinos.

Vainikolo crashing over for five tries. An early exit from the cup at the hands of St Helens and inconsistency in the league, dominated by Minor Premiers Leeds Rhinos, left the Bulls, by September, chasing the runners-up spot. This was attained with an emphatic, 11–try romp against a St Helens team missing seven regulars. The Bulls benefited from a dramatic match at Warrington where a narrow 28–27 win gave the team the ideal preparation for the play-offs.

A qualifying semi-final at Headingley was to turn out to be Bradford's best performance of the season, with them smashing the Rhinos' 100 percent home record with a stylish 26–12 win. Former South Stand hero Iestyn Harris tormented the home side all night in a typical ferocious derby. The now annual trip to Old Trafford saw the Rhinos and Bulls lock horns again. This time there was to be no happy ending as Bulls' West Yorkshire rivals dominated the titanic tussle from the start, winning 8–16.

Chapter 10 Unbelievable

Super League 10 proved to be the season that, above all others, encapsulated the history of Bradford rugby league, as the team slipped to 11th at one point, before finishing as champions. Only Bradford could show such erratic form. It has often been said on the Odsal terracing that following this club for one season is the equivalent of supporting anybody else for three years: 2005 proved that beyond any doubt.

The Challenge Cup trail had ended in disarray at the KC Stadium, where the Bulls allowed Hull to build up an unassailable 20-point lead before half-time. Even with a spirited fight-back, Bradford saw their cup dreams disappear for another year in a grandstand finish, losing 24–26. As the season progressed, injuries to key players mounted up, there were behind-the-scenes contract negotiations and the rumour mill was working overtime.

On Sunday 5 June, runaway leaders St Helens arrived at Odsal to face an injury-plagued Bradford side, not helped by the early dismissal of Leon Pryce. The Merseysiders ran in 12 tries against their depleted opponents, winning 66–4. Had it not been for Leigh's hopeless position, the unspeakable word relegation would have been swirling around the Odsal bowl.

Bulls player Ben Harris against St Helens at Odsal.

Jamie Peacock tries to break through the St Helens defence.

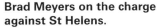

Brad Meyers on the charge against St Helens.

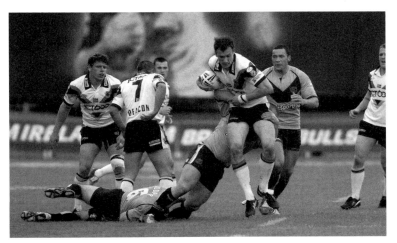

Bradford's captain Jamie Peacock takes the ball through the Rhinos defence of Matt Diskin and Chris McKenna.

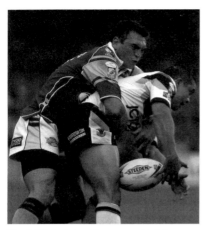

Paul Deacon gets grappled by Rhinos' Kevin Sinfield.

Stuart Fielden locked in combat with Rhinos' Richard Mathers and Kevin Sinfield.

Loan signing Adrian Morley.

Head coach Bryan Noble and his staff did not panic and started to work a miracle, turning the demoralised squad into contenders. In rugby league, as in life, miracles do not happen over night. Gradually players came back from long-term injuries, performances improved and confidence returned.

Although six of the first-team squad had decided to leave the club at the end of the season, a bond was developing that would ensure that this group of young men would go their separate ways as champions. The last eight Super League games were won, the team amassing 385 points in the process. The run included a 42–10 victory over the defending champions, Leeds, shaking the very foundations of Headingley. The Bulls, written off in June, were in serious contention.

As if to confirm the club's intentions, Adrian Morley was signed on loan from Sydney Roosters for the rest of the season. The final league match was at Knowsley Road, where Saints were in party mood after securing the Minor Premiership the week before. The Bulls proved to be the ultimate party poopers, winning 32–18. Leon Pryce showed the St Helens faithful what they could expect from him in Saints colours the following season, having already signed for the club.

The play-offs saw London easily despatched before cup-winners Hull visited Odsal. In a sensational display of speed and skill, the Bulls humiliated the Black and

Diving over the line for a try is Bradford's Stuart Fielden.

Whites 71–0. The final hurdle on the road to a fifth successive Grand Final was the Bulls' nemesis of the modern era, St Helens, in a do-or-die encounter back at Knowsley Road.

The epic contest was not decided until the 73rd minute when Shontayne Hape glided over for a try, the Bulls winning 23–18. History was made that October evening, St Helens becoming the first Minor Premiers not to reach the Final, while Bradford celebrated being the first club to secure a Grand Final berth from third position.

Old Trafford proved to be the Theatre of Dreams as the rampant Bulls put the Rhinos to the sword. With scrum

Lesley Vainikolo shows his immense power as he strides for the try line.

Shontayne Hape just after scoring his try in the Engage Super League Play-off eliminator against St Helens at Knowsley Road.

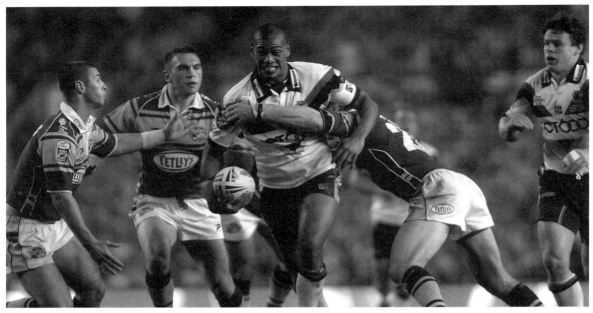

Bradford's Leon Pryce feels the brunt of the Rhinos' defence.

Try scorer Lesley Vainikolo goes over the line despite the efforts of Rhinos' Andrew Duneman.

Bradford Bulls celebrate winning the Super League Grand Final over Leeds.

half Paul Deacon orchestrating play, Adrian Morley outstanding in the forwards, Leon Pryce taking the Man of the Match award and the interchange tactic between Ian Henderson and the ever-popular Robbie Paul completely altering play and confusing a tired Leeds defence, the Bulls earned their fourth Super League crown.

The predicted exodus of players saw seven of the squad depart. For 2006, Brian Noble recruited

Brian Noble lifts the cup to celebrate winning the Super League Grand Final.

Jamie Langley struggling to get past a Tigers player.

experience in Marcus Bai, Marcus St Hilaire, Chris McKenna, the charismatic Stanley Gene and Terry Newton. From the club's highly productive academy system another crop of youngster were champing at the bit, eager to establish themselves in the game. Brett Ferres, Jamie Langley, Karl Pryce, Matt Cook and Sam Burgess were all to figure as the season unfolded.

The season's opener could not have come any bigger than the World Club Challenge against the pride of the southern hemisphere, Sydney team Wests Tigers, at the

The Bulls celebrating their record-equalling third World Club Challenge win.

Captain Iestyn Harris holding up the trophy.

newly named Galpharm Stadium in Huddersfield. The squad for the match showed six changes to that which had so confidently lifted the Super League title only three months earlier. Brian Noble again proved the master tactician, leading his charges to an astonishing 30–10 victory, thus lifting the trophy for a record-equalling third time. Stuart Fielden proved his accolade as the best forward in the world was justified, while Stanley Gene picked up the first medal of his career and gained instant cult status among the fans. That February evening was the last match as chairman for Chris Caisley who, in his 17th years at the helm, had turned the old Bradford Northern from a part-time outfit into a highly professional club, steering them through their most successful period in their history. Peter Hood took over the chair and within months would find himself in at the deep end.

As the league campaign rolled on, and the Bulls were challenging for top spot, a heavy defeat against St Helens ended any aspirations of Challenge Cup success.

In June, Odsal was shaken to its foundations when Brian Noble, a life-long club servant as player, assistant coach and head coach, left to take the helm at Wigan. He immediately took assistant coach Phil Veivers with him, leaving young Steve McNamara to take up the reins. Within a month, Stuart Fielden joined his former mentor at the JJB Stadium for a world-record transfer fee.

The off-field activities suddenly appeared to be dominating the headlines. Chief executive Gareth Davies led an exodus from the back office, while on the park, McNamara had quietly steered the team to the play-off semi-final against Hull at a hostile KC Stadium. In what is now the norm for Super League semi-finals, the contest ebbed and flowed, with no quarter given and none asked. Only a cruel call by the officials prevented a sixth successive visit to Old Trafford.

For the centenary season, Steve McNamara started to stamp his own personality on the club by assembling his own team, bringing in talented forwards David Solomona, Glenn Morrison, Chris Feather and gifted centre James Evans, as well as new back-up staff. Faces change but the same rules apply.

Bradford Bulls have never had the luxury of having a Russian billionaire to back the club; generally, they have been starved of substantial financial investment. Fortunately, structures first put in place by Australian coach Brian Smith have been the foundation for the club's unprecedented success: achievements built on meticulous planning and superb teamwork, both on and off the field.

Bradford Bulls' head coach Brian Noble leaves to join Wigan.

Bradford Bulls' new head coach Steve McNamara.

Peter Hood at the press conference to unveil the new head coach of the Bradford Bulls.

Team of the century

When the idea of trying to pick a team of the century was first mooted, I thought that I would easily be able to reel off a list of players who have both thrilled the fans and had a significant part in making our club great. How wrong could I be?

John Downes

A packed out Odsal stadium for a match against the Leeds Rhinos.

Eddie Tees' kicks won many matches, but this goal and six more were not enough to win the match against Castleford at Odsal.

For the more I thought about each position, the more complicated it got. A hundred years is a long time in rugby league and the rules, styles of play and training regimes have changed so much over the years that a player who was great in his day would not necessarily be a success in another era. Should scoring records be the be all and end all? Does longevity of service come into the reckoning? Do you pick a team on individual merit, or do you pick a team that you think would play well on the park? The fact is that you must set your own criteria, or say to hell with it and just go with your heart.

First of all, let us just go through some of the candidates you might pick in your team and hopefully set the debates and arguments going by offering some alternatives to some of the more obvious potential players for the team.

At full-back we might have Gomer Gunn, Welsh international and full-back in the historic game against the New Zealand 'All Golds', George Carmichael of the 1940s, or record goal-kicker of his era Eddie Tees. Do we go for the more obvious Keith Mumby or Joe Phillips, who once kicked 14 goals in a game and went on to be club chairman? Would Terry Price, one of the best kickers of a ball in open play the club has seen, come into the reckoning? How would Michael Withers compare?

On the wings, would the leaping Eric Batten or diving

David Barends hands off the legendary Clive Sullivan in 1978.

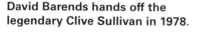

Ernest Ward holds up the League Championship Trophy in 1944.

David Barends feature, or the flying Berwyn Jones? Do you go for the power of Lesley Vainikolo, Tevita Vaikona and Jack McLean, or the more subtle skills of David Redfearn, or Mike Lamb with his excellent sidestep? Or would you feature Malcolm Davies, who scored more than a try per game in a rapidly weakening side in the late 1950s?

In the centre, would you pick a young Stanley Brogden, who made his debut in 1927 as a 17-year-old but was sold to Huddersfield to balance the books? Tommy Winnard, the first star signing of the 1930s and scorer of over 1,000 points, must come into the reckoning alongside Ernest Ward, captain of club and country, who was also a record points scorer. How would these be balanced against the likes of Paul

Nigel Stephenson falls to a strong tackle from Eric Hughes in the Premiership Final against Widnes at Swinton.

Newlove or Shontayne Hape combining pace with power?

Stand-off presents a similar quandary. What about the wily Teddy Melling of the 1920s, magical Welshman Willy Davies of the successful 1940s side who would ghost past the opposition, speedy Ian Brooke or the classy Nigel Stephenson? Would you pick Ellery Hanley at stand-off or in the centre? Would John Woods, who once scored 38 points in a game, or Henry Paul, who not only jointly holds the club goals in a match record, but also once kicked 35 goals on the trot and still holds other records, be in your team?

Scrum half would present a particular problem for me for I share with Dave Hatfield a particular favourite in the shape of Bak Diabira, who fooled them all with his tricks in the late 1960s and early 1970s. Tommy Smales was hugely influential just after the re-formation in 1964 while Barry Seabourne, Alan Redfearn, Deryck Fox and, of course, the hot-stepper himself, Robbie Paul, all come

Dynamic scrum half Bakary Diabira turns the Leeds defence inside out during the derby game at Headingley on 16 September 1967.

into contention. What about record scorer Paul Deacon, still only 27 and now captain of the side?

In the engine room of the scrum, how do you quantify the tough-as-teak qualities of first tourist, prop Harold Young, against the scrum dominance of open-side prop Frank Whitcombe? What about the enforcing qualities of Jimmy Thompson, Kelvin Skerrett, David Hobbs or Jim Mills, against the sheer power and athleticism of Stuart Fielden, or is a place there for Paul Anderson for, if nothing else, that hand-off on poor Gary Connolly?

Another major change in positional play has been at hooker, where the job of ball-getter has been replaced by ball player and runner. Choices here range from Vic Darlison, Milan Kosanovic and Keith Bridges, who could all guarantee a good share of the ball, against the more rounded skills of Tony Fisher and Brian Noble, who combined the ball-getting role with a more mobile style. Then came the half-back-style hooker and the unique Jimmy Lowes, who transferred from scrum half to ball-getter and back to the half-back style with ease.

In the second row we have one of the toughest decisions of all. How could you leave out Trevor Foster MBE, who came to Odsal in 1938, scored tries in two successful Challenge Cup Finals, played for Wales and the Lions, coached the side, was a director and was still club official timekeeper up until his death, aged 90, in

Brian Noble gains valuable yards against Hull KR. Keith Mumby is the Northern player behind him.

Frank Foster meets new signing Glen Beaumont at Odsal in 1969.

2005? Against all that there are many candidates for the second-row berths. We retired the shirt of Karl Fairbank in his honour. Jeff Grayshon performed with success before moving up to prop and Terry Clawson provided all-round skill both with the ball in hand and with his kicking skills. Paul Medley destroyed many a side with his wide running and I for one will never forget Roy Powell's big hand reaching out of a ruck of players to score versus Leeds at Valley Parade. Danny Gartner was a non-stop player in attack and defence. Frank Foster and Alan Rathbone could strike fear into opponents and Jamie Peacock developed into a world-class player at the Bulls.

Loose forward is another position where we have had a range of styles, from the emphasis on running of Bob Haigh to the more defensive style of Len Casey. The 1940s and early 1950s were dominated by Ken Traill, while Cumbrian Johnny Rae complemented the skills of scrum half Tommy Smales in re-establishing Bradford Northern as a force to be reckoned with. John Pendlebury played well behind the forceful pack of the early 1990s and Steve McNamara's footballing ability helped take the side to its first Super League title in 1997. Mike Forshaw developed into an international and Brad Mackay showed us the skills that made him an Aussie international.

Ken Traill receiving the ball from Donald Ward with Eric Batten in support, against Halifax in the 1949 Wembley Cup Final.

Full-back

In the first season of the Bradford Northern club, Gomer Gunn appeared in every game, having stayed with the club as it was reborn at Greenfield. Gomer was a former Welsh international rugby union player who had come north for the 1903–04 season and had been a star of the side at Park Avenue. Gomer left the club in 1908, playing first at Wigan and then at Keighley before returning at the very end of his career in 1918.

Sadly, between the first season and the eventual move to Odsal, no one player dominated the full-back position, the nearest being Ted Oliver, who captained the side in the 1920s. Indeed, every season between 1908 and 1934 saw at least three and sometimes four or five players in the role. In 1934, George Carmichael changed all this, signing from Hull Kingston Rovers and remaining the first-choice full-back, apart from the

Full-back Gomer Gunn, pictured back left, after his move to Wigan.

Joe Phillips, the attacking Kiwi full-back, who played for Bradford Northern between 1950 and 1956, amassing a massive 1,463 points including 661 goals. He once scored 14 goals in a single game against Batley in 1952.

occasional full-back appearance of a young Ernest Ward, until his last season, 1949–50, when he shared the role with Bill Leake. George made 473 appearances over 16 seasons between 1934 and 1950. He kicked 409 goals and scored 18 tries and was full-back in the 1947 and 1948 Challenge Cup Finals at Wembley.

As George Carmichael's career came to an end, chairman Harry Hornby went on a recruiting mission to New Zealand and signed a young New Zealander, Junior All Black Joe Phillips. Joe was a superb attacking full-back who once scored four tries from full-back in a game versus Halifax. His six years as a player saw him overhaul Ernest Ward's career points record and his goal tally of 616 was not overtaken until Keith Mumby broke the record in 1983. Joe once kicked 14 goals in a match against Batley in 1952, a solo record which lasted until Henry Paul equalled it in 2000. He played between 1950 and 1956, making 232 appearances, and scored 661 goals and 47 tries. Joe became club chairman in 1964 when Northern rose out of the ashes.

The next player in my list is the enigmatic Terry Price. The ex-Llanelli and Wales rugby union ace full-back and kicker was also a Great Britain rugby league tourist to Australasia. He was a great kicker of the ball who gained maximum yards from penalties, in contrast to the present-day trend to go for safety. Terry made 123 appearances

Vaughan Thomas, Bakary Diabira and Terry Price intently watch their teammates from the stand.

Eddie Tees is presented with an award by Mrs Phillips, wife of the late Joe Phillips, whose points and goals-in-a-season record he had broken in 1972.

from 1967 to 1971, scoring 384 goals and 25 tries. He left Northern to kick for the Buffalo Bills in the NFL.

Although he had only a short career with the club, Eddie Tees' goal-kicking feats make him a stand-out player and he held the goals-in-a-season record for a time with 178. Signed from Barrow, Eddie played for three seasons between 1971 and 1973, including the Challenge Cup Final at Wembley in 1973. He made 96 appearances, scoring 401 goals and 11 tries.

When Eddie Tees took the shock decision to end his Odsal career after the defeat by Australia in 1973, the club, rather than enter the transfer market for a more established full-back, handed the number one shirt to a 16-year-old Bradford product, Keith Mumby. Keith made a sensational debut in November 1973 versus Doncaster, scoring 12 goals and a try. Known as 'Sir Keith' to the Northern faithful, Keith played in a total of 588 games for Northern over an incredible 20 seasons, scoring 779 goals and 84 tries. Viewed by many as one of the game's best ever full-backs, Keith also toured three times with Great Britain, appearing both at full-back and centre.

Stuart Spruce signed for the Bulls in 1996 from Widnes and made 134 appearances, scoring 67 tries before injury ended his Bulls career in 2001. 'Sprogger' was both an excellent attacking full-back and organiser of his defence, as well as having a real skill in

A young Keith Mumby holds the ball before taking a penalty at Batley.

Stuart Spruce.

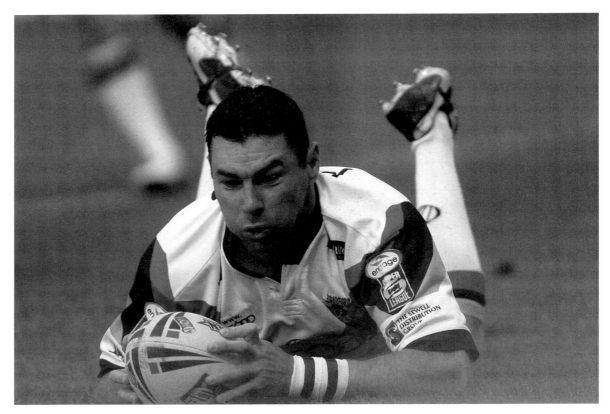

Michael Withers scoring his first try of the match against Warrington in the Super League semi-final.

conventional tackling and being able to smother the ball to stop an opponent grounding it in try-scoring situations.

My next choice is a stand-out player who signed for the Bulls in 1999 from Australian club Balmain Tigers. Mick Withers is a great organisational full-back but also appeared at centre, wing and stand-off. Mick was Australian Young Player of the Year in 1994. He played 184 games for the Bulls, scoring 118 tries, 18 goals and four drop goals. He transferred to Wigan Warriors for the 2007 season.

Along the way I have recalled others that stand out for a whole variety of reasons. Bill Leake, who played in the 1949 Challenge Cup Final, I was told, had a toe missing on one foot. In my youth, I watched New Zealander Bill Seddon perform with considerable skill in the latter half of the 1950s and then Tony Beevers and Ghulam Abed, who occasionally played full-back before the demise of the club in 1963, along with such names

Alan Rhodes scores against Bramley at McLaren Field in 1970.

as Eddie Trumble and Arthur Hattee. In the 1960s, Erroll Stock came over from Queensland and became the fans' favourite with his stout defence and exciting attack. Alan Rhodes, too, performed with credit in the late 1960s, as did South African Mick Brown. There was Stuart Carlton in the 1970s, who occasionally played full-back, and John Green, who played in the early 1980s, followed by Martin Potts, Darren Moxon and Ian Wilkinson. And then there was poor Alex Green, a half-back who was chosen at full-back against the mighty Wigan in the 1992 Challenge Cup semi-final at Burnden Park. 'Poor lad', to quote the late Eddie Waring. To come to the present day, we look to have a rising star in Michael Platt.

Michael Platt on the ball.

The Wingmen

A classic photograph of Eric Batten leaping over Williams of Leeds at Headingley on the Wednesday following Northern's Challenge Cup Final victory over Leeds at Wembley.

Now we focus on some of the game's entertainers; the men who regularly score tries, sometimes running round the opposition, sometimes running over them and, in one player's case, by jumping over them. Eric Batten, son of the legendary Billy Batten, was the man in question, timing his run to commit the would-be tackler and then hurdling the bemused opponent. Eric joined Northern in the 1943–44 season from Hunslet and stayed for eight seasons, making 233 appearances and

Kiwis Jack McLean and Bob Hawes.

scoring 165 tries. He appeared in the 1947, 1948 and 1949 Challenge Cup Finals, scoring a try in the 1949 Final against Halifax. Eric toured with the Lions in 1946, playing in four full international games.

Emlyn Walters is a good example of someone whose career was affected by the war years, but he still managed to score 173 tries for Northern over 11 years at the club, from 1939 to 1951, and in two of those seasons he crossed the whitewash over 30 times.

In August 1950, Northern signed a wingman who was to prove to be the most prolific try-scorer in the club's history. Jack McLean was already a New Zealand All Black when Northern chairman Harry Hornby captured his signature as one of five Kiwis who were to play for the club. Jack was both fast and strong, and could read the game so well that many of his tries were scored from interceptions, leaving the defence flat-footed and only able to see Jack racing away. In only his second season he scored 63 tries in 46 games, following up with 59 the following year and 52 in 46 games in 1953–54. Injury meant he only scored 16 in 22 appearances in 1954–55, but in 1955–56 he returned with 60 in 41 games. He scored 17 hat-tricks, four in a match eight times and five in a match six times. In total, Jack scored a remarkable 261 tries in 221 games. In addition to his try-scoring feats, Jack was extremely

Malcolm Davies a prolific try-scoring winger. When he was sold to Leeds for £3,000 in 1957, thousands of supporters stayed away. He returned to Odsal nine months later.

Berwyn Jones races clear of the Doncaster cover.

durable, playing in 133 consecutive games between April 1951 and April 1954.

The next choice of wingman is one who played for Northern at a time when the team was on something of a downward slide, in the late 1950s, when financial troubles meant that players were sold to balance the books. Malcolm Davies was a Welsh international wingman of the late 1950s. He played for Northern for four seasons between 1956 and 1960 and scored a remarkable 96 tries in 91 appearances including a hat-trick against Australia in 1957. He was actually transferred to Leeds during 1957 but returned the following season to continue his try-scoring exploits, scoring 45 tries in 35 games. One can only speculate as to the number of tries Malcolm might have scored in a more successful Northern team.

The late 1960s saw the coming together of a wing pairing balancing the searing pace on one flank of ex-sprinter Berwyn Jones, who scored 35 tries for Northern in 65 appearances before moving on to a brief spell at St Helens and retirement from the game, and the bustling style of Australian George Ambrum.

David Redfearn dives over for a typical try.

Moving on, in the three seasons between 1970 and 1973 the team had one of the most productive wing pairs in their history. In season 1971–72, Mike Lamb, a signing from Leeds, on the right, and David Redfearn, on the left, scored 35 tries each. Mike had pace, a tremendous side-step and flair, and in these three seasons scored a total of 77 tries. David was on the left wing and was the top try scorer of the early 1970s. After signing from the Shaw Cross club in Dewsbury, he went on to play in 470 games for the club, scoring 240 tries and four goals. He was a Great Britain international on seven occasions and a member of the World Cup-winning side of 1972.

In the latter part of the 1970s, David Barends joined the club from York. David was an exciting South African wingman who was famous for both his diving tries and the fact that he was the only non-British player to tour with Great Britain. David made 202 appearances

David Barends hurdles a York defender in a style reminiscent of Batten.

Phil Ford attempts to go through a gap against Hull KR.

Jon Scales scores the final try for the Bulls in the Challenge Cup semi-final at Huddersfield.

Tevita Vaikona.

between the 1977–78 and 1982–83 seasons, scoring 70 tries. The forward-dominated approach of the 1980s and early 1990s meant that Northern wingmen struggled to get into double figures in the try-scoring stakes, with only Phil Ford, Gerald Cordle and, briefly, Brimah Kebbie springing to mind as notables, each with their own different style. Phil Ford was the elusive-stepping type who made seven appearances for Great Britain in the late 1980s; Gerald Cordle, the powerhouse who intimidated his opposition and made one appearance in a Great Britain shirt; and Brimah Kebbie, who had out-and-out pace.

And so we move into Super League. The Bulls have built up a tradition of wingmen who possess both power and pace. John Scales, with his tries in the 1996 Challenge Cup semi-final, coupled with carries from acting-half to take the weight off his forward colleagues, set the trend, but the two men who epitomise this tradition most of all come from the same Pacific island of Tonga.

Tevita Vaikona, known as 'The Chief' or just 'TV', was the powerful wingman and Kiwi international who joined the Bulls from Hull Sharks in 1998. 'TV' played 166 games for the Bulls, scoring 101 tries, and appeared in four Grand Finals, three Challenge Cup Finals and two World Club Challenge matches.

The second of these powerful athletes is Lesley

Lesley Vainikolo goes over the line despite the efforts of Rhinos' Andrew Duneman.

Vainikolo. Known as 'The Volcano', Lesley signed from Australian club Canberra Raiders in 2002. Lesley made his debut for the club in that year's World Club Challenge win over Newcastle Knights. On leaving the Bulls to play for Gloucester Rugby Union Club he had scored 149 tries in 152 appearances. His last try was scored at Headingly in his last game for the Bulls, a 36–14 win. He appeared in four Grand Finals, three World Club Challenge games and one Challenge Cup Final.

Other wingmen who spring to mind for a variety of reasons are Hawes and Knopf from the 1950s, Levula, Thomas and Litten from the 1960s, Francis, Austin and Gant from the 1970s and into the 1980s, followed by a young Henderson Gill and Hugh Gumbs, who is still plying his trade as player-coach at Baildon RU.

Rudi Francis takes Leeds' David Smith on the outside as Trotter backs him up.

Centres

Of the centres who have represented the club over the years, some have been try-scorers, some have been expert providers for the wingmen outside them and others have been outstanding in preventing their opposite number from unleashing their wingman down the line.

Bradford-born Stanley Brogden was arguably one of the finest of his day. Sadly, the best of his career was not at Bradford but at Huddersfield, to whom he was sold, aged 19, after just over 60 performances for Northern in which he scored 18 tries and kicked five goals.

Tommy Winnard is the next candidate. A record signing from St Helens for £385, Tommy was the first 'star' signing of the 1930s as the team became more successful. The first to score 1,000 points for the club, he played a total of 253 games, scoring 167 tries and kicking 278 goals between 1933 and 1944. Tommy was also an England international.

Signing in 1943, Bradford-born Jack Kitching was a schoolteacher at Thornton Grammar School in his day job. He played for the club until 1951, forming, with Ernest Ward, one of the best partnerships ever to wear the red, amber and black. He played 171 games and scored 48 tries and two goals. He played in the Challenge Cup-winning sides of 1947 and 1949 and toured with the Lions in 1946.

Ernest Ward, probably the most well known of Bradford Northern centres, captained the successful team of the 1940s and also captained England and Great Britain, making a total of 41 international appearances. Ernest signed for Northern in 1936 from Dewsbury Boys' Club and played a total of 391 games, kicking 538

Tom Winnard, here seen playing for England v France at Thrum Hall in 1937.

Local lad Jack Kitching, seen here in his Bradford Northern training kit.

Donald and Ernest Ward in action against Leeds on 14 December 1940 (Ernest with the ball).

goals and scoring 117 tries. He was transferred to Castleford in a player-coach role in 1953. His 34 points in the game against Liverpool Stanley in October 1945 was a record which stood for the next 40 years.

After signing for Northern from New Zealand in 1952, Bill Seddon spent the early part of his Northern career in the centre, playing almost the whole of season 1955–56 as centre to Jack McLean, with the centre/wing partnership yielding 72 tries. A good all-round footballer who played for 10 seasons before retiring in 1963, he appeared 262 times, scoring 30 tries and kicking 292 goals.

Young centre Peter Roe races away on the run which brought his try against Leigh at Hilton Park.

Northern's skipper Bernard Watson breaks clear and races for the Huyton line at Alt Park.

Moving forward to the early 1970s, we come to Peter Roe. Peter was a Yorkshire County and England Under-24 centre who signed from neighbours Keighley for the 1975–76 season. He was a fiery but extremely talented player who, but for a knee injury which ended his Northern career, would arguably have gone on to greater honours. He played a total of 99 games, scoring 33 tries.

Bernard Watson signed from Leeds in 1970 and was one half of a wing/centre partnership with David Redfearn that scored a total of 54 tries in the 1971–72 season, with Bernard contributing 19 of those tries to David's 35. He combined good evasive skill with a fair turn of speed and resolute defence. He had the honour of playing at Wembley in the Challenge Cup for Leeds in the famous 'watersplash' Final in 1968 and in Northern's defeat by Featherstone in 1973.

In the 1980s we come to Steve McGowan, or 'Stick' as he was affectionately known to the Northern faithful. He played for the club between the 1983–84 and 1993–94 seasons, having signed for the club from Leeds where he played in the colts team. Steve will be best remembered by many for the hat-trick he scored at Knowsley Road in the first Northern victory on that ground for many a long year. He played a total of 242 games for Northern, scoring 107 tries and kicking six goals.

Paul Newlove.

Scott Naylor is tackled by a Widnes defender.

A couple of years prior to the start of the Super League era, Paul Newlove was a record signing from Featherstone in 1993. Regarded by many as the best centre of the early 1990s, he made 68 appearances for the club in a relatively brief career at Odsal, scoring 60 tries, including 35 in his first season in 1993–94. A Great Britain international, Paul was transferred to St Helens in 1995 in a deal which saw three players moving from Saints to provide the backbone of the new Super League side.

And so we come to Super League. Scott Naylor was one of the toughest right centres in the Super League, signing for the Bulls from Salford Reds in 1999 and playing until the end of the all-conquering 2003 season. He played a total of 147 games for the club, scoring 62 tries and wrapping up one after the other of the 'star' centres that he came up against.

The Bulls' 2007 side contains a player who must be ranked among the top few centres in the world today. Shontayne Hape, a signing in 2003 from the New Zealand Warriors side, has great evasive skills allied with an ability to read the game and be in the right place at the right time. 'Shonny' is a New Zealand

Shontayne Hape on the attack.

Ralph Winnard gets the ball away against Keighley at Lawkholm Lane.

Dave Stockwell looks to put his winger away against Leeds at Odsal.

Stuart Carlton is carried off by teammates Eddie Tees and Peter Small, together with physio Ronnie Barritt.

international and, until the start of the 2007 season had made 106 appearances, scoring 73 tries. His partnership with Lesley Vainikolo on the Bulls' left-hand side attack has proved one of the most lethal in Super League and a developing understanding with David Solomona suggests that the Bulls' left flank will be even more deadly in future.

Derek Parker crosses for his second disallowed try, again for an alleged forward pass.

Roger Simpson heads through a gap in the Wakefield defence. Roger was to stay at Odsal for 10 years as a player and a further 10 years as a groundsman.

There are others who have served the club in the centre who may well come into the reckoning of fans' favourites. Joe Mageen and Ralph Winnard both served the club well in attack and defence in the 1950s. Brian Lord, Willie Walker and Geoff Wrigglesworth come to mind from the 1960s, Ian Brooke played both centre and

Darrel Shelford.

Matt Culland.

Danny Peacock beats Steve Prescott to score at Wembley.

stand-off, as did David Stockwell. In the 1970s there were Les Gant, Stuart Carlton, Graeme Evans and Phil Ward, and in the 1980s there were Derek Parker, Ellery Hanley and Richard Davies, leading on to Steve Parrish, Steve Donlan, Roger Simpson, Tony Marchant and the rock-solid Darrel Shelford, who later spearheaded the club development team. In Super League we have Matt Calland and Danny Peacock, who ran as good 'lines' as anyone I've ever seen, and would you pick Graeme Bradley as a centre or stand-off?

Graeme Bradley.

Stand-off

We now move on to the stand-off position where, pace or guile, or indeed a combination of both, are paramount in deciding who is deserving of a place in the team of the century.

Our first candidate is Edward 'Teddy' Melling, who signed for Northern in 1920 from Batley. He played a total of 286 games, scoring 33 tries and kicking 120 goals, before leaving to join Broughton Rangers in 1928. A talented half-back, it was unfortunate for Teddy that he played for the club at a time when financial constraints meant that many players who showed talent were sold to balance the books, and it was something of a miracle that Northern managed to hold onto him as long as they did.

The next in line is William T.H. Davies. Willie Davies was a star signing by chairman Harry Hornby on finishing his teacher training at Carnegie College in Leeds. He had played at Swansea Rugby Union Club with his cousin, Haydn Tanner, appearing while schoolboys against the mighty All Blacks in an 11–3 victory in 1955. A teacher by profession, he taught at both St Bede's and Bingley grammar schools. Willie played in all three of the Challenge Cup Finals in 1947, 1948 and 1949, winning the Lance Todd Trophy as Man of the Match in 1947. He was once described as being 'perfectly balanced and having a change of pace and direction sufficient to carry him through the smallest gap like an elusive ghost'. He was a creator rather than a try-scoring stand-off, scoring 35 tries in 210 appearances for the club and kicking two goals. He was a Welsh international and toured with the Lions in 1946 to Australia and New Zealand.

In the early 1950s, Len Haley, a signing from

Cleckheaton RU, held the stand-off role. These were the days when the outside backs were scoring tries galore and Len's clever footballing skills played a big part in supplying the type of ball they needed. He was a member of Northern's table-topping side that took on Wigan in the Championship Final at the Leeds Road ground in Huddersfield in 1952, eventually losing a tight game 13–6. Len was a tremendously loyal club man, playing for the club for 13 seasons from 1951–52 to 1963–64. He played in 288 games, scoring 38 tries and kicking one goal.

Signing from Halifax soon after the club's re-formation in 1964, David Stockwell played an important part in the early days of the fledgling club. David went on to make 337 appearances over the next 13 seasons for Northern, scoring 38 tries before retiring during the 1976–77 season. A Yorkshire County representative, he possessed a great side-step and turn of pace to go through the gap and put his supporting player away. David could also play centre and it was in this position that he appeared in the 1973 Challenge Cup Final against Featherstone Rovers.

Northern's stand-off Nigel Stephenson fires out a pass in the 6–0 win over Widnes in the John Player Trophy Final at Headingley on 5 January 1980.

In the late 1970s, Northern signed Nigel Stephenson from neighbours Dewsbury. Nigel did not possess great pace, but was a classy, creative stand-off in Northern's double league title wins in 1979–80 and 1980–81. In his three seasons at the club, from 1978 until 1981, he scored 14 tries and kicked 36 goals, with 16 drop goals.

Although John Woods only played for Northern for a relatively short time, he left his mark on the club with some record-breaking appearances. John signed from Leigh in 1985 and, in his two seasons with Northern, he scored 421 points in 62 games with 21 tries, 167 goals and three drop goals. John scored a record 36 points in a game with five tries and eight goals against Swinton in 1985.

Our next candidate, Ellery Hanley, joined the club initially in the late 1970s but the main part of his Odsal career ran from 1981 until 1985. He was a player who had pace, guile and also power, and it was no wonder that he went on, during his Wigan career, to become one of the greats of the game. While some of Ellery's earlier games were played in the centre, it was from stand-off that he scored his remarkable 52 tries in the 1984–85 season. Ellery played 118 games for Northern, scoring 90 tries and 81 goals, with one drop goal, before transferring to Wigan. He was a Great Britain tourist in 1984.

Ellery Hanley scores.

Robbie Paul passes the ball.

Robbie Paul shows his delight at winning the Challenge Cup against Leeds in Cardiff, 2003.

Known as 'the hot-stepper', Robbie Paul made his first-team debut for Northern in 1994. He became the youngest-ever captain of a Wembley side in 1996, when he also became the first player to score a hat-trick of tries in a Challenge Cup Final. He also won the Lance Todd Trophy as Man of the Match in that game. Robbie could spin, turn and be through a gap in an instant, either scoring himself or putting a colleague away. He went on to hold the honour of being either club captain or team captain in four more Challenge Cup Finals, six Grand Finals and two World Club Championship Finals. Robbie made 305 appearances, scoring 156 tries and

Robbie and Henry Paul with the Challenge Cup outside City Hall.

three goals. He was also a New Zealand international, playing over 20 times for his country. He will also feature in the choice for scrum half, having played equally well in that position.

Robbie's older brother, Henry Paul, joined the Bulls from Wigan in 1999. He was a brilliant individual and team player, forming a deadly partnership with both brother Robbie and rising star Paul Deacon. Henry played a total of 100 games, scoring 32 tries and kicking 416 goals. A Lance Todd Trophy winner as Man of the Match in the 2000 Challenge Cup Final at Murrayfield, Henry also once kicked 14 goals in a match against Salford in 2000 and was the holder, for a time, of the record number of goal-kicks and points in a season for the Bulls and the world record of consecutive successful kicks at goal with 35.

Someone else worthy of consideration is a player who, he is quoted as saying, left the club so that he could make the stand-off berth his own. Leon Pryce played in his favoured stand-off position in only around a third of his 148 appearances for the Bulls, but started the 2004 season at stand-off in a string of games, including the World Club Challenge against Penrith Panthers, in which he scored a great solo try. This run of games ended with the signing of our next candidate and

Leon Pryce.

Leon never started a game at stand-off again before he left the club for St Helens.

Finally we have the present incumbent of the stand-off role at the Bulls, Iestyn Harris, who, although not having as quick a turn of pace as in his time with the Rhinos, can still destroy the opposition with his pinpoint passing and astute kicking game.

In case I've missed your particular favourite out, I've thought of a few more who've worn the number six shirt over the years. Derek Davies and Lance Davies played in the 1950s and early 1960s and Garth Budge came over from Queensland, served the club with credit, married the chairman's daughter and is still living in the area after a distinguished coaching career in youth rugby. David Treasure starred in the 1973 Challenge Cup semi-final against Stevo's Dewsbury, while Mick Blacker was a gritty number six who went on to earn a testimonial with the club. And let's not forget Ken Kelly, an import from St Helens, with his long hair and probing style, and Johnny Wolford, who treated the Northern faithful to

Iestyn Harris on the ball.

David Treasure ploughs through the mud at Odsal.

some great footballing skills. Ian Slater came and might, on a different timescale, have formed a great partnership with Paul Harkin. Russell Smith could have decided that refereeing was his calling after a spell in the Northern Colts. For Roger Simpson and Neil Summers, Super League came a little too late in their careers, but both gave us some memorable moments, not least that 'try' at Wakefield 'scored' by Neil. The Wakefield fans still haven't forgiven us for that!

Scrum half

Donald Ward signed for Northern from Dewsbury junior football in 1938 and went on to play for the next 13 seasons, scoring 62 tries and 26 goals in his 357 games. Donald was the kind of tough competitor who never took a backward step and helped to steer one of the most talented sides in the club's history around the field.

One of the smartest signings for the 'new' Bradford Northern side in the early 1960s was Tommy Smales. A clever scrum half, Tommy was signed for the club in the 1964–65 season from Huddersfield and guided Northern's new side to their first cup win in the Yorkshire Cup Final in 1965. He formed a great understanding with loose forward Johnny Rae, and baffled many a defence with the move which saw him darting off from the scrum on the open side, shielding the 'ball', while Johnny disappeared round the blind side with the real ball. Sadly, joining the club in the twilight of his career, he played only 61 times, scoring 13 tries.

Wily, creative captain, Tommy Smales, in 1966.

Following Tommy was a player whose change of direction and tricky ball-handling skills made him one of my own all-time favourites. Bakary Diabira signed for Northern in the 1966–67 season from Constable Street Youth Club in Hull. He was a magical scrum half who could turn on a sixpence, sometimes confusing even his own side, such was his speed of thought. He played a total of 131 games, scoring 14 tries and three goals for the club before leaving for the seaside and leading Blackpool Borough in some of their better times.

Barry Seabourne signed from neighbours Leeds in the 1971–72 season. A scrum half more in the Tommy Smales mould than Diabira, Barry was a good organiser and leader, playing 128 games for the club between

Bak Diabira is led from the field by physio Ronnie Barritt and Les Thomas as coach Harry Street looks on.

1971–72 and the 1977–78 season, scoring 16 tries and 53 goals with 20 drop goals. Barry led the side in the club's first Wembley appearance for 24 years, captaining the side in the 1973 Challenge Cup Final against Featherstone Rovers. He later returned to coach Northern in the 1980s.

Waiting in the wings when Barry left Northern was a player from the Batley area, whose style perfectly suited the type of team that new coach Peter Fox was building. Brother of wingman David, Alan Redfearn was a strong, direct scrum half who was almost like having an extra

Barry Seabourne passes to Colin Forsyth at Wilderspool.

Alan Redfearn breaks from the scrum to be confronted by Norton, the Hull loose forward.

forward on the field. This was ideal for the style of play that Fox was to produce over the next few years as the side became renowned for winning the midfield battle. Alan signed for the club in the 1972–73 season from Shaw Cross and played for the club for 12 seasons before retiring in 1984. He made 244 appearances, scoring 51 tries and 32 drop goals. Alan was a member of the double Championship side in 1979–80 and 1980–81 and became a Great Britain international in 1979.

It was ironic that the man who was to fill Alan's boots was the same man who had vied for the scrum half role 10 years previously. Paul Harkin was a tricky footballer

A young Paul Harkin cuts through the St Helens defence.

whose style was in almost total contrast to that of Alan Redfearn and who was, in some ways, a victim of the style of play that Northern were to exhibit over the next few years. He was transferred to Hull KR, for whom he went on to star in Cup Finals over the next 10 years in what was a great time for that club. Paul returned to Northern in the 1986–87 season and played a total of 117 times in his two spells for the club, scoring 20 tries, six goals and 22 drop goals.

Peter Fox looked once again to his Featherstone roots to bring his namesake (but no relation) Deryck Fox to the club in the 1992–93 season. He was a great organisational scrum half and excellent goal-kicker who made 107 appearances for Northern, scoring 17 tries, kicking 303 goals and 16 drop goals before a serious knee injury severely hampered his career. While at Odsal, he appeared once for Great Britain in 1992.

Our next candidate arrived at the club in the early 1990s as an untried teenager from New Zealand and was not considered for the first team in his early days because coach Peter Fox thought that he was too small. Only two years after making his first-team debut in 1994, Robbie Paul had installed himself as automatic choice for scrum half. He is also featured in the stand-off section where his considerable achievements are listed. Robbie was also a New Zealand international, playing over 20 times for his country.

And so we come to the present incumbent of the scrum half role at the Bulls, Paul Deacon. Wigan born, Paul was signed in 1998 from Oldham Bears as an academy player. Paul is a superb organiser with an excellent kicking game and is also a prolific goal-kicker, who overtook Keith Mumby's long-standing points and goal-kicking records in 2006. He has appeared in one Challenge Cup Final and all six of the Bulls' Grand Finals, winning the Harry Sunderland Trophy as Man of

Deryck Fox feeds the scrum against Warrington.

the Match in 2002. To the end of the 2006 season, Paul had made 257 appearances, scoring 64 tries and kicking 848 goals and 21 drop goals. He is a Great Britain international, having played 12 times for the British Lions plus four Lancashire and seven England appearances. Paul is the present Bulls captain.

There are others that some of you might have as your favourite. Gwylfor Jones and Roy Goddard played with merit in the sides of the early 1950s, when Northern finished top of the league and won the Yorkshire Cup. I remember Geoff Higgins, Alan Lancaster and Graham

Paul Deacon on the ball against Leeds.

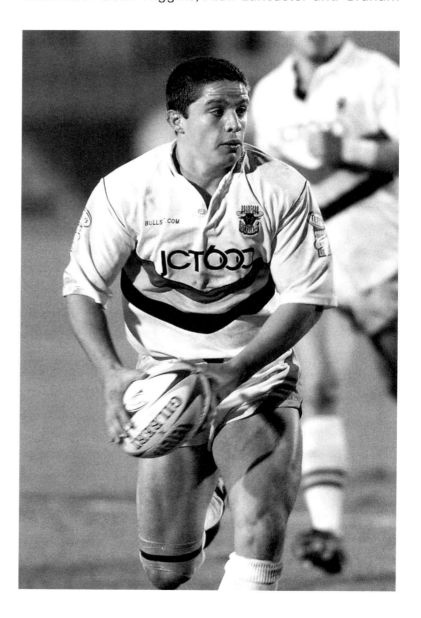

Oddy in the late 1950s and early 1960s. Goal-kicking scrum half Dean Carroll played in the early 1980s, as did another Featherstone lad, Dale Fennell, while Wakefield chief executive Steve Ferres also played with some credit. Perhaps the unluckiest scrum half that I can remember was poor Terry Holmes. Terry was an outstanding player for the Welsh RU team and came to rugby league too late in his career. His debut (at Swinton of all places – no extra bums on seats there then!) was marred by a shoulder dislocation and his subsequent comeback game, in an A team match at Odsal, I believe against Batley, produced the same injury. A long lay-off and successful operation meant that Terry eventually played 32 games in the 1986–87 season, scoring eight tries. He was one of the best passers of a ball that I have ever seen – if only he'd have come over to rugby league earlier in his career, who knows how good he could have been, either as a scrum half or loose forward. Ironically, it was a knee injury rather than his shoulder that caused his retirement after just four games in the 1987–88 season.

Props

One of the positions that has changed most during the last 100 years is that of prop forward. In the early days, when it was 'first there formed the scrum', the prop could have been any player, but gradually, as the rules changed, the props became enforcers and cornerstones of the scrum, the ones who decided whether the scrum should hold or wheel and who gave the hooker a chance of winning the ball. For this to happen, the props needed to be shorter and broader than the six-foot-plus, more athletic Super League version. This makes the choice of props for a team of the century even more difficult. In choosing, there will be even more of a need to look at the player's performance within the era in which they played.

Our first contender is Harold Young, who signed in 1926 from Whitehaven. Harold played prop, second row or loose forward and was Bradford's first tourist to Australia and New Zealand in 1928. Because of the club's cash-flow problems, he offered himself for transfer and was sold to Huddersfield in 1929. He returned to Bradford, playing in the first two seasons back at Odsal in 1934 and 1935.

Frank Whitcombe became one of chairman Harry Hornby's major signings. Frank was the epitome of the 'old-fashioned' prop. He signed on 23 December 1938, from Broughton Rangers, and became the cornerstone of Northern's great pack in the 1940s. A Welsh and Great Britain international, Frank played 331 games, scoring 35 tries and one goal. He was a tourist in 1946 with the Lions.

Local lad David Hill also epitomised many of the qualities of the blind-side props of his era. David was a tough-tackling, uncompromising prop from Queensbury

Harold Young, Northern's first-ever British Lions tourist, in 1928 before his move to Huddersfield. He returned to the Bradford club in 1933.

who won Yorkshire County honours. Playing from 1965–66 until 1974–75, David appeared in 210 games, scoring 12 tries.

Captain of the double title side of 1979–81 and the Premiership winning side of 1978, Jimmy Thompson signed from Featherstone for the 1977–78 season. Once again, Jimmy was signed by coach Peter Fox as a cornerstone for the pack. Jimmy played from 1977–78 to

David Hill scores.

The 'Flying Wedge' of Grayshon,
Thompson and Forsyth.

1980–81, appearing in 145 games and scoring 11 tries
and one drop goal.

'Selwyn', as he was affectionately known to the
Northern faithful or, to call him by his real name, Ian
Van Bellen, signed from Huddersfield for the 1977–78
season. Although he only played for three seasons,
appearing in 86 games, he was a member of the double
title-winning team and also appeared in the 1978
Premiership-winning side. Ian was a great character,
frustrating the opposition and often gaining penalties
for his side as that frustration boiled over. He scored
seven tries and kicked two goals in his Northern career.

Colin Forsyth signed for Northern in August 1974. He

**Ian Van Bellen tries to break
through the Wakefield defence.**

had starred for the York club against Northern, being one of the main reasons why York had triumphed 21–12 on the day. The Bradford directors acted quickly, negotiating a transfer, and Colin was quickly signed. He was deceptively quick for a big man and was devastating near to the opponent's line. He appeared 154 times in a Bradford shirt, scoring 57 tries.

Only a select list of players have started their career as a back and then graduated from loose forward to second row and eventually to prop forward. In completing this journey, such players bring with them the accumulated skills of their previous positions. Jeff Grayshon was a great example of this. When he signed in October 1978 from Dewsbury, he had already graduated to the back row but ended up not only as the pack leader and captain of Northern, but also as open-side prop in the Great Britain side that defeated Australia in 1978. He had a brief spell at Leeds but came back in March 1987. When Jeff left for Featherstone in July 1988 he had played 255 games, scoring 37 tries.

Kelvin Skerrett on the charge.

Kelvin Skerrett signed for Northern in 1987 from Hunslet as a free agent, building up a reputation as a fearsome, uncompromising prop. Kelvin appeared for Great Britain on eight occasions while with Northern. He left Northern for Wigan in 1990 at the end of a contract which again left him a free agent, and he was one of the first players to have this type of contractual agreement in rugby league. Kelvin played 92 games for Bradford Northern, scoring 19 tries.

Policeman Jon Hamer joined Northern as a colts player from Halifax amateur side Elland and made his first-team debut in the 1985–86 season. Jon proved one of the most reliable and hard-working props in Northern's history and it was fitting that he made the transfer from the Stones Bitter Championship into Super League and played in the 1996 Challenge Cup

Big Roy Powell is brought down by the Castleford defence.

Final. Jon gained a testimonial with the club and retired in 1996, having played 247 games and scored 14 tries.

David Hobbs came from Featherstone in 1986 as a second row but soon moved up to the front row, where his clever football brain and ability to offload out of the tackle caused problems for many a team. David was both player and player-coach for Northern and played in 224 games, scoring 30 tries, 501 goals and 32 drop goals before retiring in 1994.

Another player who started as a second row man but graduated to prop was Roy Powell. Roy was the epitome of the workaholic forward who never took a backward step. He was hard but fair, a gentleman both on and off the field. One of the classic moments of the 1990s was Roy's big hand stretching out through a mass of Leeds players to score the clinching try against the Headingley outfit at Valley Parade in 1993. Roy played from 1991 until the 1995–96 season, notching up 132 games, scoring 13 tries and kicking one goal.

The next candidate is a man who played at the club for over 10 years, Brian McDermott. Brian exemplified hard work winning through. In his career with Northern and then the Bulls, he appeared in all the positions in the pack apart from hooker and even went on loan to Doncaster, but he preferred to come back to Odsal to fight for his place than make the move a permanent one. Signing for Northern from Eastmoor ARLFC after a spell in the Royal Marines, where he shone as a boxer, Brian went on to play 219 games for the club, scoring 42 tries.

Paul Anderson, or 'Baloo' as he was known to the Bulls crowd, signed for the Bulls from Halifax, having fought his way back from a serious illness which threatened to end his career. He had previously played for Leeds, but had not reached his potential at either of his first two clubs. A massive man, Paul was just

Brian McDermott.

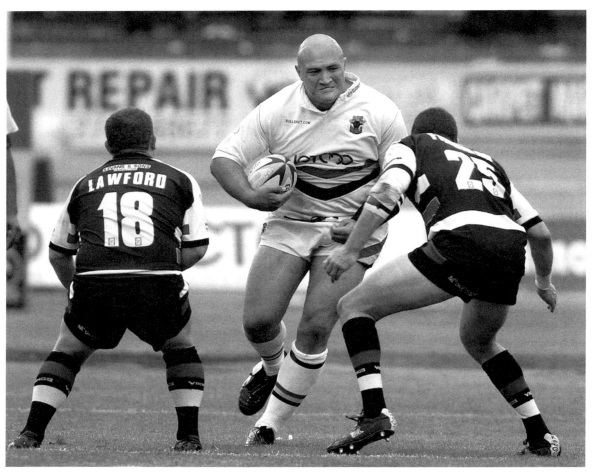

Paul Anderson eyes up the Widnes challenge.

Stuart Fielden in action against Huddersfield's Eorl Crabtree at the Odsal Stadium, Bradford.

beginning to hit the straps when tragedy struck again and he had to spend almost all of 1998 on the sidelines with a serious knee injury that required a reconstruction. Undeterred, Paul worked hard and for the next five seasons became one of the stand-out props of Super League, gaining 10 Great Britain caps between 1999 and 2003. Who can forget 'that' hand-off on Gary Connolly in 2003? Paul played a total of 196 games, scoring 23 tries before leaving at the end of 2004 to sign for St Helens.

The next choice was described as the best prop in the world in 2006 after his World Club Challenge performance against the Wests Tigers. Stuart Fielden joined the Bulls as an academy player from the Illingworth club in Halifax and had toyed with the idea of becoming a professional footballer. He is a perfect example to any young player of someone who listened to his coaching and conditioning staff and worked and worked to fulfil his potential. There are no short cuts in Stuart's training or playing. Stuart appeared in 247 games for the Bulls, gaining Challenge Cup, Grand Final and World Club Challenge winners' honours as well as appearing for Great Britain on 20 occasions. He was the scorer of 49 tries in his Bulls career.

And last but by no means least we come to 'Big' Joe Vagana. Joe signed in November 2000 from the then Auckland Warriors in New Zealand. A fearsome

Joe Vagana.

Ken Roberts winds his weary way up the slope after the game.

Arnie Long on the break.

Les Sellers looks for a way through the Swinton defence.

presence on the field both in attack and defence, with the added ability to offload the ball, Joe has dominated the middle of the field in many matches over the last seven years. A Kiwi international, Joe has played more than 200 games and scored more than a dozen tries, including many, he will tell you, from 40 metres out!

There are others who may be favourites to some or just worthy of remembrance. Some may recall Len Higson of the 1940s, and Phil Crabtree and George

Big Brendan Hill on the charge.

Andy Lynch being fought to the ground by Widnes' Mick Cassidy.

Sam Burgess scoring a 'try' which was disallowed.

McLean, who later became a director of the club, from the 1950s. Ball-playing Peter Goddard and enforcer Ken Roberts played with credit in the 1960s. The 1970s saw props such as Arnie Long, Brian Hogan, Mick Murphy and local man Les Sellers appearing in the front row, while in the 1980s Mick Atherton, goal-kicking Jim Fiddler and crowd favourite Brendan Hill all brought their differing skills to the team. Of the Bulls era, Jeff Wittenberg and Tahi Rehana spring to mind, and what about the latest crop of Andy Lynch and Sam Burgess?

Hooker

The hooker was traditionally the ball-getter and without a good one your team would not win the game. Now the game has evolved so much that the traditional role is gone – in fact the ball goes nowhere near the hooker in the scrum! In the present-day team, the hooker is another half-back and such attributes as a good pass off the ground and good speed around the ruck, as the 'play the ball area' is now known, are prerequisites of a good hooker. So once again the choice of a player for the team of the century is a difficult one.

Our first candidate, Vic Darlison, first played for Northern in the 1942–43 season and went on to make 249 appearances, scoring one try and two goals. A no-

Northern's coach, Trevor Foster, chats to players Mackie, Kosanovic, Scrobey and Hambling.

nonsense hooker, Vic appeared in all three of the Wembley Challenge Cup Finals in 1947, 1948 and 1949.

Norman Haley was a local lad, signing from Wyke in 1948. He was a solid, no-nonsense player who guaranteed the team a good supply of ball. He was a member of the table-topping team of 1951–52, being the only person to play in every game that season. He played for Northern until 1955, notching up 198 games.

The only Yugoslavian to play for Yorkshire, Milan Kosanovic signed for Northern in the 1955–56 season and went on to make 143 appearances, scoring 12 tries over the next six seasons before transferring to Wakefield Trinity. He combined the hooking skills needed to win the ball at that time with mobility in open play.

Tony Fisher joined his brother Idwal at the club in 1967 from the RAF and quickly established himself as a tough character at the centre of the pack. He went on tour alongside club colleagues Jim Mills and Terry Price in 1970, but soon followed Mills out of the club, being transferred to arch-rivals Leeds. The supporters at the time saw the transfer as a cost-cutting exercise and a sign that finances were tight. Tony returned to the club in the 1978–79 season when, alongside former pack

Tony Fisher is presented with the Supporters' Player of the Year award by Miss Bradford Northern, Mary Greenwood.

Keith Bridges drives in towards the Oldham defence.

Francis Jarvis celebrates with Mick Murphy.

colleague Jim Mills, he played in the victorious 'Dad's Army' side which beat Australia at Odsal.

John 'Keith' Bridges came to the club from Featherstone and was one of the last out and out ball-getting hookers. He played a crucial part in the first of the Championships in the 1979–80 season. In all, he played 60 games for the club, scoring three tries.

Local boy Francis Jarvis made his first-team debut in the 1972–73 season. Frannie was a 'full on' enthusiastic player, equally at home at hooker or in the second row. He was a great supporting player, forming a particularly good understanding with Bill Ramsey, and scored 14 tries in the 1974–75 season. In all, he made 112 appearances for the first team, scoring 30 tries.

Another Bradford lad, Brian Noble, made his debut for the club in 1979, going on to make 395 appearances

Brian Noble, Roger Simpson and Keith Mumby.

and score 33 tries. He played at a time when the hooker's role was to win the ball from the scrum, and in the latter half of his career was a half-back type player, directing the team and being mobile in loose play. As well as captaining the Northern side, 'Nobby' also gained the accolade of captaining the Great Britain side on the 1984 tour to Australasia, playing 11 times for the Great Britain side between 1982 and 1984. After retiring as a player he joined the coaching staff, eventually becoming head coach of the Bulls side which achieved Grand Final, Challenge Cup and World Club Challenge success. Brian also became Great Britain coach in this period, before leaving the club in 2006 to join Wigan Warriors.

James Lowes was an iconic player who signed from Leeds in 1996. Having started his career at Hunslet as a half-back, Jimmy was both a great organiser and defender as well as being a deadly attacker near the opponents' line. He played a total of 238 games for the club, scoring 99 tries and dropping one goal before

You'll never see this again: Bulls' James Lowes at scrum half against the Bees at Wagon Lane.

Trevor Foster meets teammates Dilorenzo and Mugglestone in the Middle East during 1944.

Peter Astbury breaks away from Rochdale's Charlie Birdsall.

'Give us a sup.' Keith Mumby reaches to take the water bottle from Dean Raistrick.

retiring after the Grand Final win against Wigan at the end of the 2003 season. He gained five Great Britain caps during his time with the Bulls.

There have been others who may stir the memories. Vincent Dilorenzo played for Northern in the 1930s and 1940s and the fact that Trevor Foster tells us that Vincent 'always demanded the ball at first receiver', shows just how the game has changed. Some may recall the 'grafting' type of hookers that Northern have had, like David Dyson, Peter Dunn and Tony 'Tiger' Handforth, while others might recall hookers like Peter Walker, Peter Astbury and Lewis Cardiss, who would fit into the more modern half-back type of player.

What does seem to be unusual is the number of local players who have worn the number nine shirt for the club over the years. Already mentioned are Norman Haley, Francis Jarvis and Brian Noble, but there is a whole host of others. The multi-talented Kevin Hutchinson showed tremendous promise before injury cut short his career. Dean Raistrick was a signing from Keighley who was busy in the loose and could guarantee a good supply of the ball, as could Jimmy Eyre and the bustling Brian Outlaw. The last two players, Gary Brentley and Glen Barraclough, were both mobile, defensively good and unlucky to be at the club at the same time as Brian Noble.

Second Row

The second row forward needs to have the speed of a three-quarter with the destructive power to break up the opposition's attacking forages on the fringes. It is one of the positions that has changed least over the years and so makes a comparison between players of the past and present more easy to perform.

Alf Mann became Bradford's first Test player when he played against Australia in two Test matches in 1908–09. He was a strong forward in both attack and defence and had a knack of scoring crucial tries. He was one of the players sold to Hull KR in 1909 in the infamous deal where Mr Bayliss, the club secretary, sold Alf and Tommy Surman, the club captain, to Hull Kingston Rovers and then disappeared with the proceeds, never to be seen again. Alf returned to help the club in 1918–19 and played for a further four years until he retired in 1922. In total, he played 171 games for Bradford, scoring 29 tries.

Foster, Dilorenzo and Mugglestone team up again at Odsal.

Our next candidate, Trevor Foster, came to the club in 1938 from Newport, South Wales, making his debut in October of that year against Hull at Odsal. Trevor was one of those special players who had skills both with the ball in hand, be it breaking through or passing the ball out of the tackle to a supporting player, and also in defence, where his athleticism allowed him to cover tackle the attacking player. He played the game hard but fair, never once being sent off in his 17-season career as a player. Trevor played in a total of 433 matches for Northern, scoring 130 tries and one goal. He once scored six tries in a game against Wakefield Trinity in 1946. He was a member of the great Bradford Northern team that played in three consecutive Challenge Cup Finals in the late 1940s, winning on two occasions. Trevor toured with the Lions in 1946, playing in one Test match against New Zealand. He also played twice for Great Britain in 1948 as well as 16 times for Wales between 1939 and 1951. After finishing his playing career, Trevor coached the team, was a director, played a major part in the re-formation of the club in 1964 and was the timekeeper right up until his death in 2005.

Terry Clawson played for the club for five seasons between 1964–65 and 1968–69. He was a clever,

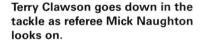

Terry Clawson goes down in the tackle as referee Mick Naughton looks on.

Dennis Trotter tries to evade the tackle of ex-teammate Stan Fearnley, now with Leeds.

footballing second row who could either burst through tacklers or offload the ball to his supporting teammates. He was also one of a select band of Northern players who have kicked over 100 goals in a season: he kicked 103 in the 1965–66. In total, Terry played 133 games for Northern, kicking 229 goals and scoring 15 tries.

Dewsbury-born Dennis Trotter made his debut for the club in the 1970–71 season. He was a strong-running, hard-tackling second row man who served the club with merit until the 1981–82 season. Dennis was in the successful Northern sides in the 1975 John Player Final versus Widnes, the 1978 Premiership Final, also against Widnes, and the Yorkshire Cup Final win against York in 1978. He was also a member of the Northern double Championship-winning sides in 1979–80 and 1980–81. He made 201 first-team appearances for the club, scoring 26 tries.

One of the best Northern signings of the 1970s, Jeff Grayshon was signed from Dewsbury in October 1978 and, apart from a spell at Leeds from October 1985 until March 1987, remained a Northern player until leaving for Featherstone Rovers in 1988. He began his Northern

Jeff Grayshon tries to break away from Ken Gill of Salford.

Karl Fairbank.

Paul Medley.

career at second row, or occasionally loose forward, before ending his Odsal career as the cornerstone of the pack at open-side prop. Jeff played a total of 266 games, scoring 37 tries, but laying on many more for his teammates as he was very adept at committing tacklers before offloading to supporting players. He was made captain by coach Peter Fox and always led the side by example.

A late starter in senior rugby, Karl Fairbank, or 'Koncrete', was one of the toughest forwards of his day, as his nickname suggests, never taking a backward step and being a tremendous tackler. However, to stereotype Karl as just the tough guy would be wrong, as he was much more than this. He was effective as a wide-running second row in his early days and could offload the ball out of the tackle, thus making him a provider as well as a finisher. In his 10 years with the club he played 332 games, scoring 102 tries. Karl also represented Great Britain on 16 occasions.

Although our next candidate originally signed as a

Danny Gartner.

teenager for the Leeds club, Paul Medley joined Northern from Halifax. He was a devastating wide-running forward with the speed of a three-quarter and the size of a bull. Time and again 'Meds' would turn a game in his side's favour. He played a total of 264 games for the club as both Northern and the Bulls, scoring 98 tries. He also toured Australia with Great Britain in 1988.

Danny Gartner arrived from Australian club Manly Sea Eagles in 2001 with the reputation of being an exemplary professional. Whether as a wide-running second row, or as a hard tackler in defence, he set the standard for others to follow. In his 84 games he scored 31 tries and never gave less than 100 percent. Danny appeared in a winning and losing Challenge Cup Final side, two winning Grand Final sides and a winning World Club Challenge side before returning home to Sydney.

Jamie Peacock, or 'JP', as Jamie was known, signed for the club from Stanningley ARL in Leeds. His early career took him to Australia and then on loan to Featherstone before he made his Super League debut in 1999. Jamie's long-striding running often caused havoc in the opposition's defence and, combined with his non-stop action as a tackler, gave him the honour of being named Man of Steel in 2003. He was made team captain in 2005 and also became captain of Great Britain, for whom he gained 18 caps between 2001 and 2005. He played a total of 207 games for the Bulls, scoring 42 tries before leaving to join home-town club Leeds Rhinos for the 2006 season.

As usual there are probably some players that haven't been mentioned that you, the reader, would consider in your side. The massive Barry Tyler played in

Bill Pattinson scores at a frost-bound Odsal. Note the 'post protectors'!

Phil Jackson offloads to Treasure.

the great side of the 1940s. Brian Radford narrowly missed selection for the 1949 Challenge Cup Final and went on to serve the club with distinction for a further 10 years. In the 1960s, the Northern side could boast the rare sight, in those days, of a black and a white South African, Enslin Dlambulo and Rudi Hasse, packing down together in the second row, which was something they could not have done in their own country because of the apartheid laws at that time. John Sykes was one of the many bargain buys from Leeds which we seemed to pick up in the 1960s and 1970s and Geoff Clarkson also touched down at Odsal for a while as one of his destination clubs in a colourful career. Graham Joyce, Graham Idle, Frank Foster, Bill Pattinson, local lad Phil Jackson and even Llanelli RU chief executive Stuart Gallacher all wore the 11 or 12 shirt with pride and will be a favourite in someone's eyes.

Loose Forward

Once again, much like the second row position, there are aspects of the loose forward's role that have remained constant over the years of change in rugby league. The emphasis between attack and defence may have changed, but speed and the ability to tackle, support and offload the ball remain essential parts of the loose forward's armoury.

The first Northern player to tour Australia with the England team in 1928 was Harold Young. He originally signed for Northern in 1926, exchanging work down a Cumbrian pit for a job in a Bradford mill. An excellent Cumberland wrestler, Harold's main skill was as a tackler and as well as loose forward he played in the second row and at prop forward. He played for just over

Tourists Ernest Ward and Ken Traill set off in 1950.

two seasons before financial worries meant that he was transferred to Huddersfield, returning to play part of the last season at Birch Lane and the first at Odsal before retiring in 1935. In total, he played 88 games for Northern, scoring 12 tries.

Ken Traill joined Northern in the 1946–47 season from Hunslet. He was a great tackler but also had the ability to make pin-point passes that would split the defence and put his support away. Ken played for Northern until the 1955–56 season, appearing in 315 games, scoring 37 tries and kicking three goals. He played in the 1948 and 1949 Challenge Cup Finals and was a Great Britain tourist in 1950 and 1954, appearing in eight Test matches.

When Ken Traill left the club, the loose forward role was filled by a number of players without anyone making it their own. Then, in 1964, Johnny Rae, a Cumbrian loose forward, signed for the new Northern side for the 1964–65 season. Playing alongside the wily Tommy Smales, Johnny formed a great partnership that fashioned more than a few tries and helped to cement the fledgling Northern side as a new force in rugby league. Johnny spent four seasons at the club, playing

Johnny Rae hands off Roger Millward in the mud.

Stanley Fearnley strides in for a try against Swinton.

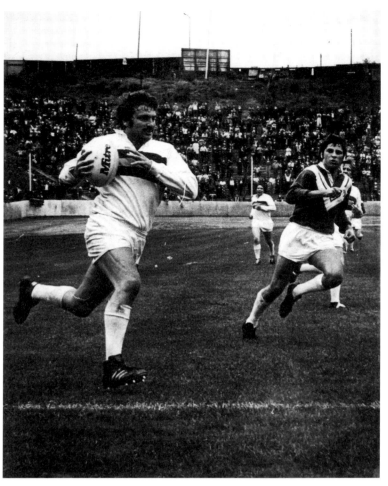

134 games, scoring 40 tries and nine goals. He made one Test appearance for Great Britain in 1965.

Son of the coach and general manager Albert Fearnley, Stan Fearnley played for Northern from 1964 until the 1976–77 season. Stan developed into a good all-round player, having both pace and footballing skills. He was a try scorer in Northern's Challenge Cup defeat at Wembley in 1973 and a Challenge Cup-winner with Leeds, to whom he was transferred in 1977. Stan played a total of 217 first-team games, scoring 41 tries.

Although Bob Haigh played much of his successful career at Wakefield Trinity and Leeds, and came to Odsal as a 'bargain buy' in the last three years of his playing life, he played a significant part in a team that was building towards being a Championship-winning side. In his second season with the club, he helped the team

Bob Haigh tries to break free from the Featherstone defence.

to a Premiership trophy win against the great Widnes side of the time by 17 points to eight, as well as the 1978 Yorkshire Cup Final win against York in his last season. In his 67 games for the club, Bob scored 18 tries.

In the 1980s and 1990s, once again we had a number of men filling the role. Good candidates for selection include Harry Pinner, a clever, ball-playing loose forward from St Helens, and the wily John Pendlebury, who was

Steve McNamara waves to Bulls fans after the semi-final win over Leeds at Huddersfield.

a master at heeling the ball from the opposition at the 'play the ball', a practice now outlawed.

And so we come to the era of the Bulls. Steve McNamara joined the club in 1996 from home-town club Hull. Although he was a ball-playing prop forward in the early part of his career, it was as a creative loose forward that he made his mark at the Bulls and was singled out by then coach Brian Smith as a future senior coach. Steve was an accomplished goal-kicker and could also prise open the tightest defence with his clever ball distribution. In his 110 appearances for the club, Steve kicked 319 goals, eight drop goals and scored 16 tries. He left the club in 2000 to end his playing career with the Huddersfield Giants and returned to the Bulls in 2005 as assistant coach, taking the reins of the senior side midway through the 2006 season.

Mike Forshaw is stopped in his tracks by Leeds' Kevin Sinfield and Keith Senior.

Mike Forshaw spent the early part of his career at Wigan before starting a journey which took him to Wakefield Trinity and Leeds in rugby league and Saracens in rugby union before he resurrected his rugby league career with the Bulls in 1997. He developed into an all-action loose forward with both great defensive skills and a superb offload game which took him to Great Britain honours and both Challenge Cup and Grand Final triumphs. Mike played 199 games for the club between 1997 and 2003 and scored 42 tries. He also made 14 appearances for Great Britain while at the club.

Of the present Bulls crop, Jamie Langley stands out as a loose forward for consideration in the team of greats. He made his debut in 2002 as a wide-running player but has developed into an all round top loose forward, consistently topping the tackle counts and

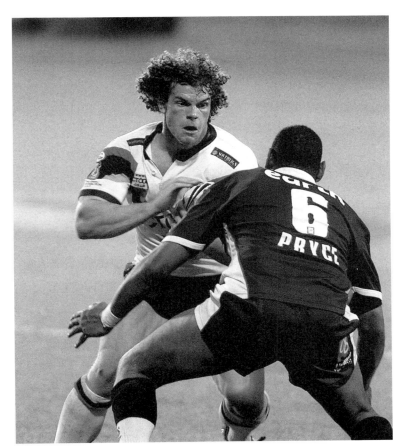

Jamie Langley trying to pass St Helens' Leon Pryce.

capable of breaking the opposition defence with his powerful runs.

As ever there are others who some may feel worthy of a vote. Billy Hutchinson was in some ways unfortunate because he was at his peak during World War Two. Who knows how good the popular Jack D. Moore would have become, for he was killed in action in 1941 when his ship, HMS *Electra*, went down off Java. Brian Radford wore the Northern number 14 loose-forward shirt (many clubs considered the number 13 to be unlucky and the loose forward wore 14) with success, but was always in the shadow of Ken Traill. Alan Rathbone was a fearless loose forward who signed for Northern from Leigh in 1981 and Len Casey had a brief spell at Odsal in between his spells at Hull KR. Australian Mal Graham was a more than useful forward who signed from Oldham for the 1986–87 season.

The Coaches

When choosing the team of the century it's also important to look at the men who fashioned the teams over the years – the coaches.

In the past, teams were chosen by the committee and there was a trainer who looked after the fitness of the players. We have record of a Mr Farrell in the early 1900s and a Mr Mereweather filling this role in the 1925 season, while Ben Gronow, who was part of the Huddersfield 'Team of all talents', was listed as 'trainer' in 1934.

The appointment of Dai Rees in July 1936 was a watershed in coaching at Bradford Northern as he had much more influence on the team selection and tactics than any before him. Dai was to remain as manager/coach for the next 24 years and in that time

Dai Rees.

Bradford Northern, winners of the 1949 Challenge Cup at Wembley. Left to right: Trevor Foster, Dai Rees (manager), Ken Traill, Bill Leake, Barry Tyler, Donald Ward, Vic Darlison, Ernest Ward, Frank Whitcombe, Ron Greaves, Alun Edwards and Willie Davies.

the team won four Challenge Cup Finals, seven Yorkshire Cup Finals and a Championship, together with numerous runners-up appearances. Unfortunately, as the stars of the 1940s and early 1950s grew older and were not replaced, Dai's magic waned and in 1960 the club felt that a new approach was needed in order to turn the club's fortunes round.

Trevor Foster was installed as the new coach but the turmoil at the club went on and Trevor's reign as coach and also as a director ended only eight months later. This train of events was to be the beginning of the end as far as Bradford Northern was concerned.

Doug Greenall, the tough, ex-St Helens centre, took brief control as player-coach in January 1961, to be followed by Jimmy Ledgard, who was Great Britain full-back in the 1950s. Jimmy never seemed to have the full confidence of the club directors, and various players were brought in to help with the coaching, including veteran Cumbrian Jock McAvoy, who tried to hold the crumbling team together from the loose forward position.

The club continued to spiral downwards and on 2 September 1961, suffered the humiliation of a record defeat of 73–5 to Wakefield Trinity in the first round of the Yorkshire Cup.

In the face of falling crowds and ever-increasing debts, Northern brought in Harry Beverley, who had taken Bramley into the First Division the year before and had a reputation as a straight-talking disciplinarian. Harry's reign was to last until November 1963, when he suddenly resigned only two weeks before 324 loyal fans witnessed the game against Barrow when Northern lost 29–0. Two weeks later the club was to announce that they could not fulfil their remaining fixtures.

As the new Bradford Northern rose from the ashes of the previous regime, Jack Wilkinson, the veteran

Ian Brooke outstrips the Leeds defence.

Wakefield Trinity prop, was appointed as temporary player coach. He was soon succeeded by former Great Britain international Gus Risman and, in 1965, the new club won its first major trophy, beating Hunslet 17–8 in the Yorkshire Cup Final at Headingley.

Albert Fearnley took over the reins from Gus Risman, aided in his coaching responsibilities by John Burnett, Stan Keilty, Alan Kellett and Mick Sullivan, and the rollercoaster ride up and down the table continued.

Harry Street's brief reign in 1971–72 took the team from 27th to second in the league, but this was not to continue. When Albert Fearnley had to take temporary charge, neither he nor Ian Brooke was able to stop the slide into the Second Division in the Wembley year of 1973. Brooke took the side back up to the First Division

Roy Francis gives his half-time talk at Odsal.

at the first attempt and for a while things looked to be on the up, but in September 1975 he bowed to pressure from the fans after a poor start to the season and resigned.

Roy Francis, who had a reputation for producing a fast-flowing style of rugby, took over, but with a background of boardroom wrangles and limited resources, Francis was able to produce only average results. Unfortunately, Roy had health problems which caused his resignation in April 1977.

After years of instability Northern needed someone that could come in and build a team capable of bringing home the silverware and they looked to Bramley coach Peter Fox to try to do both these things. Peter had just taken the Bramley team to promotion from the Second Division on a shoestring budget, building a close-knit team who outstripped their potential. Peter set about the task straight away with the signing of the hugely influential Jimmy Thompson, a sign of the no-nonsense style of team that was to come. By the end of the 1977–78 season, Northern were beating Widnes in the

Premiership Final and the success had begun. The league achievement that was to follow was beyond even the most ardent Northern fan's dreams. The club were champions in 1979–80 and 1980–81 and also lifted the John Player Trophy in 1980. Unfortunately, this was to be the peak of Northern's success at this time and when Jimmy Thompson and Nigel Stephenson, who were the guiding forces in the team, moved on, success began to wane.

The club directors were of the opinion that a change of coach was the way to arrest the slide and so decided not to renew Peter Fox's contract, which was due to run out after eight years of service. This produced a mini revolt among the players and supporters and Jeff Grayson resigned the club captaincy in protest, later moving to Leeds, where Fox had moved as head coach.

Barry Seaborne was promoted from the coaching staff to head coach in May 1985 and remained in the role until he surprisingly resigned before the opening of the 1989–90 season. Barry's most successful season was in 1987–88 when Northern finished fourth in the league and won a fiery Yorkshire Cup Final replay at Elland Road.

When Barry Seaborne surprisingly resigned on the first day of the 1989 season, experienced forward David Hobbs stepped into the breach as player-coach until a successor was appointed, taking Northern to the Yorkshire Cup Final, although new coach, Australian Ron Willey, was in place before the Final against Featherstone. The players found some of Willey's coaching methods unusual and his reign was short, lasting just six months, before David Hobbs again stood in to fill the breach, taking Northern to a Regal Trophy Final before league results took a downturn.

Once again Peter Fox came to the rescue. The club were in danger of relegation when Peter was re-appointed in

Two of the most controversial characters in rugby league, Alex Murphy and Peter Fox. 'discuss' various aspects of the game.

December of 1990. A good cup run ended with the injury-ravaged side's infamous 71–10 semi-final defeat to the all-conquering Wigan side and Northern had a real fight on their hands to avoid the drop. Only a dramatic 14–12 win over Hull KR at Craven Park saved the day, but Peter Fox had achieved what the Northern board had brought him in to do. He had avoided the drop. In the next two seasons, Northern finished second and third in the league before finishing in seventh place in 1993–94.

With Super League on the horizon,1994–95 was to be the last season at Odsal for Peter Fox. The club embraced a whole new image for the centenary season and took a new name: the Bradford Bulls. Alongside this new image, the decision was taken to appoint a new coach in the shape of Australian Brian Smith. It was to be Smith's task not only to put in place a whole new set of coaching methods, but also to restructure the club's administration. These two factors were to lay the foundations for the Bulls' success over the coming years and to start a dynasty which has yet to be broken. In the first season of Super League, Brian coached the side to the classic Challenge Cup Final against St Helens, regarded by many as the best ever Challenge Cup Final.

Brian Smith.

Matthew Elliott.

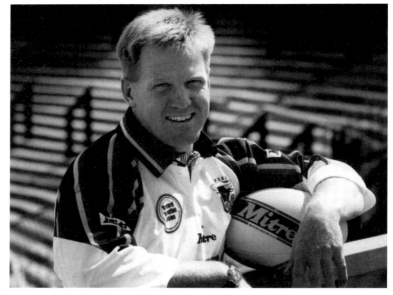

Brian Noble as a player.

Opposite: Brian Noble.

Matthew Elliott came over from Australian club St George Dragons, where he held a football development role, having had his playing career ended by a knee injury. Brian Smith had spotted the coaching potential in Matthew and appointed him as his deputy. It was Matthew, in fact, who put in place many of the coaching and conditioning plans prior to Brian Smith's arrival. Matthew led the Bulls to their first Super League championship in 1997 and to two Challenge Cup Finals: first in 1997 when they lost to St Helens at Wembley and then in 2000 at Murrayfield where, the team triumphed over arch-rivals Leeds Rhinos.

In 2001, with a growing family, Matthew took the decision to return to Australia to coach the Canberra Raiders and the Bulls dynasty rolled on, with assistant coach Brian Noble being promoted to the head coach role. Brian had served his apprenticeship under both Brian Smith and Matthew Elliott and grasped his opportunity with both hands. From 2001 until 2006, Brian coached the side to a Challenge Cup win, three Grand Final wins, three World Club Challenge wins and two Minor Premierships. The club were also runners-up in two other Grand Finals and a Challenge Cup Final during this time.

Steve McNamara at the press conference at Odsal stadium where he was unveiled as the new head coach of the Bradford Bulls.

Following Brian Noble's move to Wigan Warriors halfway through the 2006 season, once again the club looked to appoint a new head coach from within. Steve McNamara's coaching potential had first been spotted during his playing career at Hull, when he was being coached by Brian Smith and, after retiring as a player, Steve had returned to Odsal as Brian Noble's assistant. Steve had been regarded as the obvious successor to Brian Noble but perhaps even Steve himself had not been prepared for the timing of his promotion. After an initial settling-down period, the team came within an inch of yet another Grand Final appearance at the end of

2006. Steve is gradually putting together both personnel and a style of football capable of extending the Bulls' dominance of Super League.

Choosing the man to coach your team of the century will again depend on your criteria. Is he the most successful, the best at getting what seem like average players to perform above their potential on a limited budget, the best at developing junior players, or the man who produces the most exciting style of play?

Roll of Honour

Paul Richard Ackroyd
Justin L Acton
Matthew J Acton
Caleb Adams
Danny Adams
Danielle Adsetts
James Adsetts
Louise Adsetts
Alan Akeroyd
Colin Allan
Mark Algie Allan
David S Allen
Jack Ambler
Stephen Ambler
Malcolm Ambrose
Jeremy Dale Angus
David Archer
Frank Archer
Liam Archer
Andrew Charles Armitage
Lucy Ann Armitage
David Armstrong
Harry Arran
Samantha Jade Askew
Mohammad Azharullah
Henryk Bak
Janusz Bak
Jola Bak
Paul Bak
Kyle Baldwin
Mark Baldwin
Eric Balmforth
Lynne Eileen Bancroft
Paul Bancroft
David Banks
James A Banks
Paul Bannon (deceased)
Margaret Barber
Norman Barber
Ernest Barker
Margaret Barker
David Barnes
Mr Gerard Barnett
David Barok
Mavis Barr
Barrie Barraclough
Billy Barraclough

Keith Barraclough
Michael G Barraclough
Christine Ann Barrett
David Barrett
Mark Antony Barrett
Richard David Barrett
Tom Barrett
John William Barry
Michael Bastow
Courtney Battye
Makenzie Battye
C J Beaumont
Penny Bebb
Neil Beck
Geoffrey R Beddow
Alan Bedford
Andrew J Bedford
Elliott J Bedford
Harold L Bedford
Jason Bedford
Vilma Bedford
Arthur Bell
Jack Belt
Karen Belt
Rebecca Belt
Harold Benn
Sam E Bennett
John Michael Bennison
Sarah Ellen Bennison
Carol Benson
Matthew Benson
Michael Benson
Michelle Benson
Peter Benson
Dave Bentley
Douglas Best and family
John Betts
Donald Birch
Anton Birkett
Dr Simon J Birkinshaw
Simon Lee Blackburn
Daniel Paul Bland
Janet Ann Bland
Marjory Bland
Ross Andrew Bland
Terry Bland
David J Blythe

Gemma Blythe
Helen P Blythe
Peter Blythe
Simon Boddy
Anthony Joseph Bolton
Patricia Bolton
Victoria Bolton
Heidi Bond
Jon-Marc Bond
Madena Boocock
Michael Boocock
Peter W Boocock
Andrew Booth
Andrew Philip Booth
Ian Booth
Mr J Booth (Canada)
Hannah Boughton
Peter Boulton
William Boulton
Willie Boulton
Tere David Bowers
Donald Thomas Boyden
Jeffrey Bradley
Marjorie Bramhall
Paul Brennan
Peter Brennan
Robert Brent
Steven Brent
Tony Brent
Christopher Brian
Paul Brian
Colin Briggs
Graham Paul Briggs
Stuart Briggs
June Broadbent
Darren Wayne Brogan
Anita Brook
David Brook
Derek Brook
Gerald Brook
Ian A Brook
Kevin Brook
Robert Brook
Sarah Brook
Stanley Brook
Amanda Jayne Brooke
Carl Michael Brotherton

Bernard E Brown
Fred S Brown
Mr H Brown
John V Brown
Mick Brown
Mr Paul Brown
Terry Brown
Sue Brownbill
Gary Broxup
Ian Buck
Ronnie Buck
Garth Budge
Jack Burgess
Helen Burnett
Paul Burnett
Stephanie Burnett
James Burnham
Kathleen Burton
Norman Butterfield
Jenny Callaghan
Dr W H Callander
Hollie Carbine
Lee Carbine
Neville Carbine
Joe Carman
Richard Carney
Alan Carr
Gerald Carr
Mr Vincent Carr
Peter Carradice
Brian Carroll
Louise Carroll
Sarah Louise Carroll
Sophie Megan Carroll
Linda J Carter
Richard S Carter
George Cartright-Widdop
Shirley Caton
Mark Cawood
Alwyn Chadwick
Andrew Martin Chandler
Stephen Paul Chandler
Jade and Chloe Chapman
Eric Chappell
Richard A Chappell
Anthony Paul Christie
Ben Clarke
Richard Owen Clarke
Sam Clarke
Evie Coates

John Coates
Brian Collett
Brenda Colley
Gary Collier
Sandra Collier
Paul G Collinge
David Collins
Frank Collins
Karen Collins
James N Collinson
Matthew W Collinson
Stephen Connell
John Cook
Robert Cook
Paul Alan Cooper
Christine Copley
Ian Copley
Leah Corboz
Philip George Cory
Derek Cotson
Barrie Coultas
John Craven
Martin Craven
Matthew Jay Craven
Phil Craven
Miss B Critchley
Mr D R Critchley
Aaron Crossley
David Crossley
Holly Cunningham
John Cunningham
John Cunningham
Richard Czyzewski
Fred Dalby
Muriel Dale
Peter Robert Dale
Richard Daley
Robert Smith Darnbrough
Mr Valdek Davidson
Eddie Davingoff
James Lyle Davison
Christine Dawson
Paul Dawson
Arthur Deacon
Luke Anthony Deacon
William Henry Deacon
Andrew J Dean
Michelle Dean
Steve Dean
Mr Jim Deegan

Jimmy Delahunty
Shaun Delany
J Dellman
M Dellman
John Dewhirst
Gerard Dibb
Christopher Diggle
James Diggle
Carl Dignam
Adrian George Dinsmore
Carol Dixon
Claire Dixon
Joan Dixon
Peter Dixon
Joyce Dobby
Tonie Dobby
Barbara Docker
Peter Dolby
Jack Doran
Craig Allan Drake
John Drake
Walter Jeffrey Drake
Benjamin Driffield
Craig Driffield
James Driffield
Arthur Duckworth
Thomas Duff
James Matthew Duffy
Morgan Duffy
Patrick Duffy
Simon Patrick Duffy
Paul M Durkin
Andrew Earnshaw
Lee Eastbourne
Mr R Edmondson
David M Edwards
Peter N Edwards
Harry Ellis
Robert Andrew Ellis
Ronald Ellis (Australia)
Ada Ellison
Andrew R Elstub
David Emsley
Frederick William Etherington
Bill Evans
Karl Fairbank
Brian Farrell
Katie Farris
Lauren Fawthrop
Colin Firth

Jack Firth
Raymond Firth
Timothy Firth
Daniel Lee Fisher
Terry Flaherty
Bernard Patrick Flanagan
Dennis Flatt
Andrew John Foden
Dennis Foley
Irene Forrest
John Forrest
Sam Forrest
Adrian Paul Foster
Alex John Foster
Andrew Foster
Cliff Foster
David Foster
Derek Foster
Michael Foster
Simon Foster
William E Fothergill
John Fountain and Diane
Andrea Fowler
Benjamin P Fox
Peter French
Hannah L E Frost
Kathryn A Frost
Kevin P Frost
Callum Funnell
Gavin Funnell
Leonard Funnell
Jack Gardner
Alexander Harry Garner
Jane Elizabeth Garner
Mark Garner
Anthony Richard Garnett
Tony Garnett
Lisa Gayton
Barry Gibson
Richard John Gibson
Brendan Gill
David Gill
Ian Gill
Joe Gill
Kathryn Gill
Peter Gill
Mick Gledhill
Nic Gomersal
Mark Gomm
Mark Granger

Paul Gration
Edward Gratton
Jonathan Green
Malcolm Green
Peter Greenhalgh
Jim Greenough
Brett Greenwood
Chloë Greenwood
Christina Greenwood
Finley George Greenwood
Ian Greenwood
Lily Scarlet Greenwood
Martin Greenwood
Daniel Gregory
Stuart Griffin
Barry Gudgeon
Dominic Guiry
Ruan Guy
Ian Habergham
Sarah Habergham
Jeffrey Hahn
Beverley Jayne Haley
Gladstone Haley
Marjorie Haley
Steven Hall
Ray Halligan
Simon William Hudson Halling
Terence Hallsworth
Ben Hammonds
Daniel Hammonds
Martin Hammonds
Nigel Hammonds
Tim Hammonds
Brian Hanson
Dave Hanson
Stewart Hanson
Bradley Hardaker
Joseph Hardaker
Neil Hardaker
Bryan Harding
David Hargrave
Alan Hargreaves
Simon James Hargreaves
Glenn C Harland
Mark A Harland
Maurice Harland
Kenneth Harper
Christopher John Harrison
Mark David Harrison
Michael Harrison

Sam Harrison
Sheila M Harrison
Tracy Amanda Harrison
Mr Rick Hart
Norman Hartley
Paul Hartley
Harry Haveron
Robert Haxby
Peter Hayton
Andrew R Hayward
Dr Andy Haywood
Lisa M Hayward
Robert T Hayward
Darryl Graeme Helliwell
Mrs Joan Helliwell
Mr Neville Helliwell
Sheila Helliwell
Colin Richard Helm
Emma Jane Helm
Brian Hemingway
Hazel Hemingway
Bryan Henderson
Dean Edward Higgins
Nicola Jane Higgins
Danny Higson
John Douglas Hill
Mark Ian Hill
Norman Hill
Christopher Hillam
Colin Hillam
Jeremy Hillam
Mark Hillam
Simon Hillam
Mr Graham Victor Hilton
David Wilson Hindle
Raymond Hirst
Stuart Hirst
Jamie Hodgson
Matthew D Hodgson
Zack Hodgson
David J Hogg
Christine Holden
Ken Holden
Simon John Holden
Gerald and Sylvia Holdroyd
Brian Holdsworth
Bryce James Holdsworth
Dean Bryce Holdsworth
Eric Holdsworth
Jessica M Holdsworth

Walter Holdsworth
N J Holdsworth-Lofts
Stuart and Carol Holland
Betty Holmes
Keith Holroyd
Peter Holroyd
Stuart Holroyd
Jesse David Holt
John Holt
Sal Hopkinson
Susan Horsfall
Mark Howlett
Daniel Hoyle
Edward Hoyle
Philip Hoyle
Tom Hoyle
Barry Hubbard
G A Hudson
Kevin Hudson
Joe and Lou Hume
Dave Hunt
David J Hunt
Roy Hutchinson
Kevin Illingworth
Joshua David Bradley Ingham
Sophie Ingleson
Connor Jackson
Dave Jackson
Jenna Sam Jackson
Patricia Jackson
Paul Jackson
Maureen Linda Jagger
Paul Andrew Jeffery
Paul Jenkins
Philip Jenkins
Rene Jenkins
Margaret Jennings
Dean B Jepson
Andrew R Johnson
Walter Johnson
Anthony Robert Jones
Edward Glynn Jones
Michael Anthony Jones
Phillip Leslie Jones
Ian M Jowett
Ian J Keefe
Martyn Kellett
Mick Kellett
Peter Kelly
Andy Kenny

Connor Kenny
Mr Rigby Kerfoot
John David Kidd
Ellen M Kilduff
Alexander King
Andrew King
Stacey Kinsella
John Knowles
Sandra Knowles
Sandra Knowles
Mollie Krstovic
Stuart Lambert
Ross Langdale
Dawn Larkman
Marc Lawrence
Don Lawson
Mr Brian Lawton
David Lawton
David P Laycock
Ann-Marie Leach
Kenneth Leadbeater
Norman Leadbeater
Stephen Leadbeater
Wynne Leadbeater
Mr Arthur Lee
Christopher Lee
Jonathan R Lee
Kenneth Lee – Blackpool
Barrie Leftley
Francis Leith
Frank Leith
James Leith
Mr Peter Le-Talbot
Edward Levin
Ellen Levin
Eric Levin
Sami Levin
Stewart Levin
Vikki Levin
Nye Lewis
Tye Lewis
Philip Anthony Lightbody
Mr David Lightowler
Mr Dennis Lightowler
Donald Lightowler
Frank Lightowler
Jordan David Lightowler
Sarah Jane Lisle
Luke Lister
Annmarie Littlewood

Tom Lockwood
David Longcake
Jessica Helen Malik
Danny Mangham
Jenny Mansfield
Brian Manton
Neil Margerison
Christopher R Marsland
George Martindale
Mrs Christine Mason
Robert A A Mason
Tom Mason
Maureen Matthew
William Matthew
Harry Albert Matthews
Jason Matthews
Samuel Luke Matthews
Jack Maude
Philip R Maude
R Stanley Maude
Robert H Maude
Chris Mawson
Barry Maystone
Daniel Maystone
John A McCarthy
Luke McCarthy
Tom McCarthy
Catherine Jayne McGoun
Andrew McGuinness
Kevin McGuinness
Shannon McGuinness
John McHugh
James McLorinan
James Meadowcroft
Alexander Dyas Meakin
Geoff Meakin
Donald Merriman
Elaine Denise Metcalfe
James Metcalfe
Joanne Metcalfe
Robert Neil Metcalfe 22.4.58
Stevan Anthone Metcalfe
James Middlebrook
Ann Middleton
Wilf Middleton
Adam Midgley
Eric Midgley
Summer Midgley
Coleen Miller
Andrew Robert Mitchell

Helen Ruth Mitchell
James Arthur Mitchell
John David Mitchell
Nigel Mitchell
Paul Mitchell
Steven Mitchell
Mr Jonathan Mooney
Nicholas Moore
Ronnie Moore
Brian Moorhouse
Clifford Moorhouse
Natalie Moorhouse
David George Mordue
Pete Morgan
David Stanley Morris
Allison Denise Mortimer
Paul Darren Mortimer
Sophie Jean Mortimer
Steffi Elizabeth Mortimer
Barbara Morton
Robert Moss
Darren P Moulden
Saul Moulden
Steven Moulden
Donald T Muff
John Muldowney
Keith Mumby
Andrew Murphy
Stuart Myers
Dylan Naylor
Pauline Naylor
Robin Naylor
David G Neat
Ian Newsholme
Richard John Newsholme
David Newton
James Fraser Newton
Pauline Newton
Keith Nicholls
Peter Nicholls
Trevor Nichols
Mr P G Nicholson
Peter Nicholson
Paul Nicolson
John Nilen
Mary Nilen
Paul Nilen
Christopher Oakes
David Oates
Terry O'Connor

Louisa Jane Odd
Leah Ogrizovic
Christian Oldcorn
Isaac Vello Oldcorn
Oskar David Oldcorn
Edgar Oliver (Bradford
Northern)
Ray & Sandra Oliver
Adrian Paul O'Reilly
Richard Packer – Bfd Uni RLFC
Stephen Packer
Tony Padgett
The Parish Family
Harold Parker
Brian Parkin
Paul Brian Parkin
Tommy Lee Payne
David Jack Pearson
Ellen & Trevor Pearson
Alf Pedder
Andrew C Peel
Ian Craig Percival
Angie Petty
Catherine Pilcher
Christine Poingdestre
Chris Pollard
Kenneth James Pollard
Kenneth Smith Pollard
Gordon Frederick Poole
Ian Popadenis
Max Popadynec
Raymond Popadynec
Keith Porter
The Poskett Family
Darren Potts
James Pownall
John Presland
John N Presland
Robert Presto
Michael J Preston
Barbara Priestley
Charles Priestley
Colin Priestley
David Priestley
Jack Priestley
John Priestley
Keith Priestley
Kenneth Priestley
Pat Priestley
Gary Procter

Martin Pyne
Elliot Pyrah
Eric Pyrah
Keith Gerald Pyrah
Brian Quirk
Henry Ramsden
James Ramsden
P G Ramsden
Stephen Ramsden
John Ratcliffe
Mrs M Ratcliffe
Don Rathbone
Craig Raw
Mark Raw
Paul Rayner
Peter M Rayner
Stephen Dennis Rayner
Stuart Rayner
Dave Redfearn
Daryl James Redgrift
David Andrew Redgrift
Ian James Redgrift
Ian Rhodes
Ian M Rhodes
Paul Rhodes
Stephen Rhodes
Stuart Edgar Rhodes
Trevor Rhodes
Jordan James Richardson
Phil Richardson
Edward Richmond
Donna Riddell
Fred Ridewood
Richard Ridewood
Simon Ridewood
Bernard Rimmer
Catherine Rimmer
Dennis Rimmer
John Rimmer
Angie Roberts
Christopher John Roberts
Malcolm Roberts
Michael Roberts
Peter Roberts
Phil Roberts
Graham Robertshaw
Stephen Robertshaw
Cameron Robertson
Scott Roberts-Wavell
Ben Robinson

Billy Robinson (Yeadon)
Colin Robinson
David Robinson
Keith Robinson
Steve Robinson
Susan Elizabeth Robinson
Jake Barry Rochell
William Rothery
David Peter Routh
Mike Routh
Beverley Rowe
Brian Paul Rowe
Geoffrey M Rowe
Les Rowntree
Amanda Royston
David M Royston
Les Royston
Lewis Royston
Timothy Rukin
B Rushbrooke
Craig Ian Rushforth
Gary Stephen Rushworth
Trevor Rushforth
Harry Ryecroft
Gerald Samociuk
James Samociuk
Vera Samociuk
Ian Sawkill
Leigh Sawkill
George Leslie Schofield
Philip Scholes
Carl Scott
Tracy Scott
Carl B Seed
Gemma Sewell
Glenn Sewell
Julie Sewell
Andy Shackleton
Peter Shackleton
Robin Shackleton
Zara Shah
Robbie Sharkey
Steven Sharkey
Doris Sharman
Jack Sharman
James R W Sharp
Ronald Sharp
Jamie Sharpe
Wilf Sheard
Philip Shearer

Carole Sheehan
Vera Sidney
Mrs Mary Simpson
Mike Simpson-Brisbane-Aus
Alan Sinclair
Deb Skimming
Zoë Louise Skinner
Ellis J Sladdin
Richard J Sladdin
James Slimming
Miss Claire Slonimski
Miss Heather Slonimski
Miss Louise Slonimski
Mrs Pamela Slonimski
Mr Paul Slonimski
David Smalley
Albert Smith
Arnold Smith
Bryan Philip Smith
Cath Smith
Emily Jayne Smith
Ernie Smith
Graham Smith
Hannah Elizabeth Smith
Iain Smith (Rugby)
Jamie Smith
John Smith
John Smith
Jonathan Smith
Kevin Smith
Laurie Smith
Melvin Smith
Peter John Smith
Philip Douglas Smith
Sydney Fenwick Smith
Mrs Pamela Smithies
Mark Anthony Solomons
(Junior)
Dominic and Janice Speed
Allan Spencer
Mr James Spencer
Steven Spencer
Barbara Stables
Edward Stables
Adam Jamie Stanley
Peter Stanworth
Christine Stocks
Malcolm Stocks
Brian Stojkovic
Michael J Stones

Robert Stott
Barbara Strothard
Geoffrey Strothard
Heather Strothard
Martin R Sugden
Mark Sunter
Mr Bill Sutcliffe
Brian Patrick Swaine
Ben Sykes
Lauren Jessica Sykes
Dale Tabiner
Adam Tabor
Mr James Tarbotton
Adrian Taylor
Howard and Nadia Taylor
Mr P H Taylor
Sam Taylor
Peter Tetley
Joshua Thackray
Paul Thackray
Richard Colin Thackray
Mr Brian Theaker
Colin Thomas
Ryan Thomas
Alan Thompson
Janice Thompson
Philip Thompson
Stuart Richard Thompson
Michael Thornes
Andrew Thornton
Harry Thornton
Henry Paul Thornton
James Thornton
Keith Douglas Thornton
Stephen Thornton
William Thornton
Alan Tidmarsh
Ernest Tidswell
Julie Tillett
Paul Tillett
John Toothill
Lauren "Gigs" Townend
Sam Townson
Barry Tudball
Christopher Leon Tudball
Emily Tudball
Jacqueline Edna Tudball
Harry Tyas (aged 84)
Maureen Ullah
Andrew James Vahter

Ernest Varey
Andrew Vickers
Christopher Paul Wade
Dale Wadsworth
Margaret Wadsworth
Mrs Linda Wain
Mr Peter Wain
Audrey Wainwright
Jack Wainwright
John Wainwright
Robert Wainwright
Sam Wainwright
Maureen Wakefield
Carl M Walgrove
Andie Walker
Diane Walker
Helen Walker
Liam Walker
Matthew Walker
Niall Walker
Peter Walker
Frank Wall
Ralph Wallman
Graham Walton
Joan Warburton
Neil Warburton
Alicia Ward
Andrew John Ward
Holly Mae Ward
Jack Benjamin Ward
James Alan Ward
Jason Ward
John Ward
Jonathon Ward
Steven Ward
Tony Ward
Ian Watkinson

James Watkinson
Donald H Watson
Mark J Watson
Stephen D Watson
David Alan Watt
Neil Waudby
Alice Wear
Andrew Wear
Matthew Wear
Richard Wear
Terry Webb
Ronald Edgar Wells
Richard West
Alec Western
Brian Whalley
David J Wheelhouse
Barbara E Whitaker
Jordon Whittaker (from
Grandma and Grandad)
Ronnie Whitaker
Leslie K Whitcombe
Luke Whitehead
Harold Whitford
Jade Whytell
Allan J Wigglesworth
Evelyn W Wigglesworth
Dave Wilding
Graham Wiley
Peter Wilkes
Callum Scott Wilkins
Alan Wilkinson
Bev Wilkinson (Dad)
Donald Wilkinson
Keith Wilkinson
Paul Wilkinson
Frank Willey
Anthony Williams

Trevor Williams
Diane Williamson
Lionel Williamson
Daniel Willicombe
Eric Wilson
Joseph Barker Wilson
Paul Andrew Wilson
Tracy Ann Wilson
Geoffrey Winder
George Winn
Paul Winn
Stephen Winn
Harold Winterburn
Amy-Joe Wiseman
David Wiseman
Wendy Wiseman
Barry Womersley
Brian Wood
Cameron Bradley Wood
Denise Wood
Grahame Wood
Grahame Wood
Janet Elaine Wood
Kenneth Wood
Maurice Woodhead
Paul Richard Woodhead
Arthur Worley
Jeffrey Worley
Andrew Worthington
Geoff Wrigglesworth
David Wright
Graham Wright
Tom Wright
Keith Wrigley
Derek Young